S0-CEI-665

MAURICE BARING
A POSTSCRIPT

Half-Way House, Rottingdean

922.242
BAR
c.1
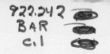

MAURICE BARING

a postscript
by
Laura Lovat
with some letters
and verse

2014

Senior Novitiate Library

NEW YORK
SHEED & WARD
1948

Copyright 1948 by Sheed & Ward, Inc.

Manufactured in the United States of America

AUTHOR'S NOTE

I would like, first of all, to say how very grateful I am to Monsignor Ronald Knox, not only for his essay on "The Effects of the Classics on Maurice Baring's Mind", but also for his invaluable help in correcting the proofs of the book for me, a task which an operation on my eyes made it impossible for me to do myself.

I must also thank all those many friends of Maurice Baring's who have allowed me to include their personal impressions of him in the book and have sent me letters or verse from him. I trust that they will forgive me if I do not mention them all here by name. I should like, though, particularly to thank Princess Marthe Bibesco for her beautiful French preface to "Passing By", and William Heinemann Ltd. for allowing me to include some letters from the book *Maurice Baring* by Dame Ethel Smyth published by them in 1938, and especially the three poems translated from the Russian which are taken from *Russian Lyrics* published by them in 1943.   *L.L.*

"Et a l'heure de ma mort soyez le refuge de mon âme étonnée et recevez-la dans le sein de votre miséricorde."

I

Memoir

by LAURA LOVAT

IT WAS hoped by those who loved Maurice Baring that a biography, including many letters, would be written about him, and I was asked to collect the letters and try to write a biography. After much thought and consultation with those who knew him best, it was agreed that the formula of a complete biography was impossible, the more so as Dame Ethel Smyth had published, in 1938, a careful and valuable record of all he had written up to his last Anthology, *Have You Anything to Declare?*, published in 1936. It is a work of love, as well as of accuracy, for, as she says in her opening sentence, she had known Maurice for forty years.

He had also written his own biography in *Round the World in any Number of Days*, *The Puppet Show of Memory*, and *R.F.C., H.Q.* These books take us to the end of the first Great War, and there are some years which must still be bridged until the date of his death in 1945. I have therefore collected a few notes, personal and impersonal, which give some impression of his life between these dates. These years were spent mainly in London, at Dulwich and finally at Rottingdean, which he made his home until 1940. After this he lived in my and my son's house in Scotland.

To collect letters has been a difficult task. In early

youth Maurice seems to have written many, in many languages and to many countries; few, alas, have been kept in the maelstrom of two wars which destroyed all Russia, most of Central Europe, to a large extent the ordered existence of English life, and cut us adrift for so many years from France. From 1920 to 1935 he was in such close touch with his correspondents that I think he preferred to visit rather than write to them. On being upbraided by me for not writing, he answered in Goethe's words "Und doch ist es in manchen Fällen, geliebte Charlotte, nothwendig und freundlich, lieber nicht zu schreiben, als *nichts* zu schreiben."

No being was more mobile than Maurice; he would start for Rome, Paris, Malta, Seville, Lisbon, Constantinople, Vienna or Berlin with the easy *désinvolture* of a man accustomed to all countries and all languages; but judging from the many bound volumes of letters which he kept, from Belloc, Prince Mirsky, Chesterton and many others, he must have written constantly to these friends. Among the material available to us are some enchanting letters preserved by careful hands, and some verse which will appear in this memoir.

In 1920 Maurice appeared a carefree man. The war of 1914-1918, in which he had served with such distinction in the Royal Air Force, was over, and though he felt the peace a precarious one, he hoped, with the fervent hope of the world, that the Continent might readjust itself to new conditions.

In 1921 he wrote his first novel, *Passing By*. Up to this date he had written a great deal, but always (except for short sketches and some children's books) from personal experience, for the theatre or in verse.

2

This, his first novel, was to him a new and absorbing interest, and from 1921 onwards he continued to write works of fiction which are now translated into many languages, and are admired most, perhaps, in France, where his clear, unaccentuated style seems in some ways to read as well, if not better, than in the original. Though apparently so effortless in their texture, so seldom emotional, so reticent in their effects, Maurice gave to these novels infinite care, and would sometimes despair both of the plots and their personages, and would appeal to friends for aid. "You should not show your writings to anyone before they are finished", wrote Tolstoy, "you would hear more harmful reflections than useful advice." "I have always done the opposite", writes Maurice, "not always with success". His mind was meticulous in its love of accuracy and he wrote only of a world he knew perfectly, and whose reactions he had long studied; for no *nuance* of this world ever escaped him. His critics have at times blamed him for writing too much of the same *milieu*—his answer was that he would not dare write of a world in which he had not lived. In this context it may be interesting to note that he wrote very little, if anything, of the life of the Court at St. Petersburg, or of the *grand monde* which was to suffer liquidation, in any of his books on Russia. It was not the Russia he knew.

He seemed so uncritical, and even detached from the life of his generation, though often its centre of gaiety and folly; but his sensitive antennæ missed no human emotion, no subtle change in the temperature or tempo of those amongst whom he lived. His reviews

3

were seldom, if ever, what he expected. ". . . has not seen the point", he would exclaim in almost piteous dismay, "he is praising me for what isn't there—I must explain". But how explain this astonishing man?

Perhaps one explanation was that with the maturity of much experience, the virtuosity of genius, the culture of great scholarship and the modesty of the saint, he maintained, until the hour of his death, the mind of a child who walked through life's joys and sorrows with a deep conviction that he was always holding God's hand. For him the end was greater than the means; nor did he know dismay. He believed that "Patience obtains everything", but it was, I think, of God's patience rather than man's that he was thinking.

I did not know him till he had been for some time a Catholic, but I infer from his letters to his relations and childhood's friends that this same quality of untarnished purity of intention, so rarely found outside the child's mind, was always present. He was received into the Church in 1909—"the only action I have never regretted" as he abruptly dismisses it in *The Puppet Show of Memory*.

His modesty over his own writing was impressive; for though he recognised it at its best with great objectivity, he was always moved at others doing so. With de Goncourt he felt "Un livre n'est jamais un chef d'œuvre. Il le devient. Le génie est le talent d'un homme mort." On hearing that Mauriac had said to Robert Speaight in June 1945 "What I most admire about Baring's work is the sense he gives you

4

of the penetration of grace", he asked me anxiously to write and ascertain in what sense the word "grace" was used, was it the theological sense, and added in his own pathetic writing "as I hardly dare think". When assured that it was so he was too moved to speak.

I imagine that after England, France and Russia were the countries in which he "lived" as he understood life. I speak of country life, and in his books on Russia one feels how steeped he was in the beauty of this country and its people. Of the aristocratic world he writes little—did he know it well? From the letter of a Russian lady of the Court, I quote the following. "You ask me to write something about Maurice in Russia. The fact is, I knew very little about him when he was there, though at times I saw him a lot. I have just read over *What I Saw in Russia* to refresh my memory, and all he speaks about in this book went on entirely *outside* my knowledge. My remembrances of him are strictly personal, so personal that they can interest no one. I met him, I believe, for the first time in St. Petersburg at Countess Benckendorff's. She said "Tu connais Maurice?" and explained at great length who I was; I had no idea who *he* was, and I thought later he was a Polish cousin; he laughed a lot and was very gay. Countess Benckendorff asked me what I thought of him after I had met him several times. I said "I don't know—he seems to be rather a freak". Then suddenly he disappeared. When he came back he had been in Manchuria for some time, and spoke a good deal of this country. He never told me why he had gone there, or what he was doing in it. I do not think that people like ourselves really interested him.

5

Suddenly he reappeared from nowhere, and we saw him a lot. He showed a wonderful insight into every Russian he met. He would just catch a glimpse of someone and say at once what that man or woman was. It was almost uncanny. From 1907 to 1914 I saw more of him. I remember when his brother, John, was expected in St. Petersburg, Maurice used to come and see me daily to tell me what I should do and say to please John. It was very touching, but I became impatient and said he had better teach his brother how to please *me*. He was like that, sometimes absurd, sometimes and even always very lovable. When John did arrive I sat between them at dinner. John said he had an apartment in Paris, and I said I could imagine what a dissipated life he led there! It was only just to say something; after dinner Maurice pounced on me, saying how could I have said such a cruel thing to John. He was so funny! Or was he *pretending* to be shocked? He was intensely interested in our country, and saw as many Russians as he could, but who outside our circle of friends, I never really knew—even those living in St. Petersburg or Moscow. I never met him at any Court reception, he never really knew our husbands or older men, who thought him strange. Despite his constant appearances and disappearances, one always met again as though one had only parted yesterday. Perhaps I saw him more constantly after we had been forced to leave our country and settle down abroad, when he was so full of kindness and understanding, and visited us every year. . . ."

Rome, 1947.

Was it more the Russians of Turgeniev's *House of Gentlefolk* or *A Sportsman's Sketch-Book* that Maurice Baring knew and loved? Reading in his books on Russia the descriptions of the newly-mown hay, the cool beauty of the river, the Easter Mass in a provincial town, the conversations with the peasants in trains, on boats and at fairs, one is inclined to think so. Though he lived to see all this life wrecked in the ruins of a totalitarian state, he never lost his faith in a Russian resurrection, for he would not hear of national characteristics changing or being forced out of existence. Perhaps his finest tribute to the country he loved so well was his magnificent translation of some of Pushkin and Alexis Tolstoy's poems, written, or rather dictated, for he could no longer write, just before his death.

This brings me to his verse. Much of it is known and most of it has been published. I do not believe that he felt he had written any great poetry, with the exception of his Elegy on his friend Auberon, Lord Lucas, and even of this he wrote to a total stranger, "October 25th, 1920. Thank you for writing to me about my poem. I cannot tell you what pleasure your letter gave me. In writing a thing like this, one knows that anything, the best even, must be inadequate, but one fears any attempt might *jar* and strike a wrong note. I am glad that you did not think so, for if you who have had the same experience were not displeased, that is all one asks. Yours very gratefully, Maurice Baring."

Of this poem T. E. Lawrence wrote, "It takes me each time I read it absolutely by the throat—so simply sincere, and grievous and splendid. . . . It is a wonderful thing, it makes me shiver."

God who had made you valiant, strong and swift
And maimed you with a bullet long ago,
And cleft your riotous ardour with a rift,
And checked your youth's tumultuous overflow,
Gave back your faith to you
And packed in moments rare and few
Achievements manifold
And happiness untold,
And bade you spring to death
As to a bride,
In manhood's ripeness, power and pride.
And on your sandals the strong wings of youth,
He let you have a name
To shine on the entablatures of truth
For ever
To sound for ever in answering halls of fame. . . .

You had died fighting, fighting against odds,
Such as in war the Gods
Ethereal dared, when all the world was young;
Such fighting as blind Homer never sung
Nor Hector, nor Achilles never knew,
High in the empty blue. . . .

And the lovely falling cadences . . . one would like to quote the entire poem.

8

And in the portals of the sacred hall
You hear the trumpets call,
At dawn upon the silvery battlement,
Re-echo through the deep
And bid the sons of God to rise from sleep
And with a shout to hail
The sunrise on the City of the Grail:
The music that proud Lucifer in Hell
Missed more than all the joys that he forewent.
You hear the solemn bell
At Vespers, when the oriflammes are furled;
And then you know that somewhere in the world,
That shines far-off beneath you like a gem,
They think of you, and when you think of them
You know that they will wipe away their tears,
And cast aside their fears;
That they will have it so,
And in no other wise;
That it is well with them because they know,
With faithful eyes,
Fixed forward and turned upwards to the skies,
That it is well with you,
Among the chosen few,
Among the very brave, the very true.

In 1937 Maurice wrote "The essence of poetry is
emotion remembered in tranquillity — the essence
of journalism is sensation captured on the wing". He
was an artist who feared his poetry falling into
"sensation captured on the wing". He felt, like Proust,
that the author had the work of the translator, that he

should pause before committing to paper "Le petit sillon qu'une phrase musicale ou la vue d'une église a creusé en nous". How much more with the greater emotions!

Of his early plays in verse he talked with little affection, but he liked some of his sonnets, shorter poems and "Stop-shorts". I do not really know what he felt about his verse. On the whole, I think he considered it very uneven; but he knew himself to be an unrivalled translator; that his genius for languages was greater than a natural gift, that he could think and create in the mind of the language rather than translate it into words; but here again his scholar's mind allowed no slipshod *"pis-aller"*, often to his sorrow; far sooner would he leave the original beauty unmarred.

Of his classical competence it would be impossible for me to speak, but Mgr. Knox has written of the influence of the classics on Maurice Baring's mind in a short statement which appears in this memoir.

Maurice was no lover of "Higher education" as it is now understood. He learnt, after a sound education, "in the air, from, by, through the air—like Russians used to. The less print, education and press—there you will find the greater culture", as he writes in 1930. "People will always read what they want to read, listen to what they wish to listen to; many who have no learning develop vision, even over things they know nothing about." Against this, those who, though educated, failed to admire great scholarship, and ignored culture from whims or fads, drove him to desperation; though as he grew older he became more patient with what he believed were phases of thought, doomed to be ephemeral.

In 1930 after living at Pickwick Cottage (Dulwich), Gray's Inn, North Street and 18 Cheyne Row, Maurice bought a small semi-detached villa called Half-Way House at Rottingdean. Its exterior was only remarkable for its similarity to other houses in Steyning Road, but its interior was very different. From a wide rush-floored passage, one stepped into a room with a piano in a deep bow window, full of books and scrap-books and comfortable chairs, with lilies and roses growing in at the very windows, and one quickly revised one's first impression of red brick and stucco. Here Maurice made for those he loved a perfect home, and in it he lived in great serenity until illness (*paralysis agitans*) struck him down. He entertained many friends, lending it to the tired or the sick; filling it with the young, who could never be too noisy or fatiguing for him; sometimes obliterating himself wholly for those in great sorrow; but making it for all who knew him, from subalterns in the Brigade of Guards to the great English and Continental authors, musicians and actors of the day, a place of "green pastures". I believe he loved Half-Way House most, because of the possibility it gave him of offering hospitality. It is almost impossible to exaggerate Maurice's generosity to friends, and, sometimes almost disconcertingly so, to total strangers. His gifts were enhanced by their suddenness, though birthdays, Christmasses and Easters were strictly remembered. A hat, a cheque, a first edition of great value, a sewing machine, a love poem, a racing debt would be pressed at any and all times into the hands of those he loved. My children and grandchildren, before entering his room, were carefully warned to admire nothing, lest it should be given them. To a sick friend he writes "Only tell me of the books which *don't* arrive".

Above the book-room, from which so many books were given, was his chapel which he cherished with infinite care and filled with many rare and beautiful things, and where Mass was constantly said. When he was told that the bomb which fell on the house in 1942 had entirely obliterated the Chapel as well as half the house, his one regret was that the Chapel had suffered most; but as in all personal losses he never referred to it again. Perhaps I might here say that to Maurice Baring's complete resignation was added the stoic ability to dismiss from the mind that which makes life unendurable. "You must make up your mind whether you wish to live or die, and as it appears that you are unable to die, you must now concentrate on living", he wrote to a friend after a great bereavement. This stoicism masked much sorrow, and later in life great physical suffering, and made it possible for him to amuse others, even to the end, by his fantastic and wholly unaccountable wit; a perfect example of Chesterton's words "A light touch is a mark of strength and not weakness, in spiritual as in bodily things".

The peculiarity of his humour is difficult to recapture and at moments tested his nearest and dearest—some examples have become well known, and such thistledown becomes heavy when recorded, and yet without it much that was an essential part of Maurice's mind is lost. To a friend who invites him to his wedding in Sussex, he answers "I will certainly come to the wedding, dressed as the Duc de Reichstadt if you like".

On being asked to a country house, where many of his friends stand anxiously expecting him at the front door, he arrives on a bicycle, in a straw boater, which he removes as he salutes his hostess and his friends, and gaining speed, disappears not to be seen again till the following day, when he is found sitting at the dinner table.

To a friend on the eve of the 1914-1918 war, who was in the War Office Secretariat, he telegraphs (curiously enough from Vienna) ''Feel all could be settled if we really got together. Signed, Franz Josef'', and to a gentleman who mistakes his identity and excuses himself on the grounds that he thought Maurice was "Mr. Godavari" he sweeps a low bow and answering with much conviction "I *am* Mr. Godavari" he hurries past. But memory fails one in trying to recapture these stories.

Maurice was a patron of the arts, in the most agreeable sense of the word. The work of a famous musician would take him half way across Europe, he would hurry to Italy to see Duse act, or to France to listen to Sarah Bernhardt. He had a genius for admiration.

He seldom missed a Classic race, and to the delight of all his racing friends, could, till just before his death, repeat the names of all the Derby winners in chronological order from the first Derby run in 1786.

He read in all languages, and kept copious notes of passages he admired till writing became impossible, and he had to dictate them. These notebooks are a revelation of his astonishing versatility and intimate

13

knowledge of most of the classics of Europe and much contemporary literature. In 1944 he wrote to his friend, Sir Ronald Storrs, "I finished not long ago reading the complete plays of Shakespeare from A to Z. I found on this re-reading many astonishing things; e.g., a complete and final description of the battle of France (1940) in *Pericles*". This reference to his note-books makes me (and all who knew him) think of his "*Gepäcks*"; these are small but fat, or sometimes thin, volumes; "literary luggage", as the name implies, into which he pasted on blank pages, poems or prose from the literature of all nations, cut ruthlessly from the parent book. He would give these to his friends; no two would be alike. They culminated in his anthology, *Have You Anything to Declare?*, which he gave to the world—the last work he published.

Maurice's illness began in 1937 at a moment when one might truly have said of him, in the words of his own Sonnet *The Prince Errant*:

"I am the Prince of unremembered towers
Destroyed before the birth of Babylon;
And I was there when all the forest shone
While pale Medea culled her deadly flowers.

I heard the iron weeping of the King,
When Orpheus sang to life his buried joy;
And I beheld upon the walls of Troy
The woman who made of death a little thing.

I heard the horn that shook the mountain tall
Where Roland lay defeated: and the call

That fevered Tristram whispered to the sea,
And brought Iseult of Cornwall to his side,
I saw the Queen of Egypt like a bride
Go glorious to her dead Mark Antony."

Did Maurice realise this aspect of himself? I think he did.

In 1936, realizing how ill he was, he consulted many doctors and tried most painful cures, alas! with no result. He writes from Rottingdean, "I am in London from Monday till Thursday, having what is called 'treatment'. The doctor asked me if I could still understand simple sentences. I said 'Yes, I could read words of one syllable, like the Queen in *Alice in Wonderland*'." In 1937 he writes—

My body is a broken toy
Which nobody can mend
Unfit for either play or ploy
My body is a broken toy;
But all things end.
The siege of Troy
Came one day to an end.
My body is a broken toy
Which nobody can mend.

The years passed and his illness, with all its attendant misery and helplessness, increased relentlessly, but I find in a note-book opened after his death, and dated 1941—

My soul is an immortal toy
Which nobody can mar,

An instrument of praise and joy;
My soul is an immortal toy;
Though rusted from the world's alloy
It glitters like a star;
My soul is an immortal toy
Which nobody can mar.

He continued, with the obstinacy which characterised so many of his actions, to try cure after cure, however great the torment involved.

In 1938 it was evident that war must break up Europe. Maurice believed that Munich was only a pause. He wished to visit his many German friends while it was still possible, especially the Fräulein Timme, sitting old, fragile and apprehensive behind their *"Zimmer Linden"* in Hildesheim, where he had studied German as a young man, and of which he has written with such infinite grace in the French language. Letters alone could be sent to them, apologising for his inability to reach them. They were expecting him, he knew. After this he waited in great distress of mind, for what he foresaw would be the end of civilization (as his generation had known it) in Europe. He knew men; and had seen already three wars at close quarters, the Russo-Japanese, the Balkan war and the 1914-1918, and he had suffered from the pro-Boer attitude of the French during his years at the British Embassy in Paris; for though so much a cosmopolitan, his deep patriotism was the constant background of his mind. In the Russo-Japanese war he had experienced and shared the fate and fortune of the Russian soldiers, and he had later nursed in the cholera camps of Constantinople.

16

His service to the Royal Air Force in the 1914-1918 war has been described by Marshal of the R.A.F. Lord Trenchard in his last tribute to his staff officer— in *The Times* of 17th December, 1945:—

"Among my notes that I wrote many years ago, I found the following. Major Maurice Baring was on the staff of Headquarters, R.F.C. He had met me when I first landed in France. I had always intended not to keep him as I did not know him, but the very first day he showed me his complete lack of self-interest, his complete honesty, and his wonderful loyalty to Sir David Henderson and others. He was a genius at knowing the young pilots and airmen. He knew more about what mattered in war and how to deal with human nature, how to stir up those who wanted stirring up, how to damp down those who were too excitable, how to encourage those who were new to it, and in telling me when I was unfair, more than any other man I know. He was a man I could always trust. He was my mentor and guide, and if I may say so, almost my second sight in all the difficult tasks that came in future years. In the words of a great Frenchman —Marshal Foch—"there never was a staff officer in any country, in any nation, in any century like Major Maurice Baring." He was the most unselfish man I have ever met or am likely to meet. The Flying Corps owed to this man much more than they know or think. His *R.F.C., H.Q.* should be read and re-read even partially to understand this great man. He never once failed me and only once lost his temper with me, though I must have tried him highly. All the juniors had confidence in him and all the seniors loved him.

It was he who brought the tone of "service" into the R.F.C. and brought into it altogether a feeling of doing service to help other men and save lives in the Army on the land and in the Navy at sea. I can pay no higher tribute; words fail me in describing this man."

When war broke out in 1939 Maurice was at Rottingdean, and already more or less bedridden, but I was with him on those hot days in September and we wheeled him over the lawn to cut off the heads of over-flowered roses that they might flower once again. It was warm, a St. Martin's Summer, and he spoke of planning the border for the following year, but the next summer came, and though the garden was fuller of roses than ever before, his windows had been shaken by gunfire, and the noise of air-raid warnings had become unendurable.

At a moment's notice, owing to the intolerable pain the sirens caused to his nervous system, he arranged to leave Half-Way House and come to Scotland, as he believed for a few months only, until the armies had got farther from the coast; but this was not to be, and he remained there, a loved and honoured guest, from August 1940 until his death in 1945. His existence had changed; for from this date onward he remained in constant pain within four walls, in a lonely part of the Highlands.

The house was called "Eilean Aigas", and was on an island in the river Beauly; a place of rare and unexpected beauty. Others have told of Maurice's enormous erudition, of the wit and brilliance of his conversation, but perhaps I knew him best in the last five and a half years of his life as a lover of small children, of

18

unimportant and neglected people, of minor episodes in the potpourri of war-time life, of fantastic nonsense and laughter and gaiety, so far flung despite so much suffering that at times one followed him with difficulty. I also knew his stark understanding of sorrows great and small.

His thought at times seemed to travel as swiftly as light, nor could it always be expressed in speech. This to some extent was a barrier (or so he thought) between himself and the scholars he loved and revered for their learning. (Who will ever forget him doing crossword puzzles?)

It was also a curious phenomenon in a man who had heard all the classical music of the world that he was unable to play by ear or from print "Three Blind Mice", yet could, and did play in the manner of Beethoven, Chopin, Schubert, Brahms, or any musician whose music he knew, with a virtuosity which enchanted and often deceived the late Sir Donald Tovey, and exasperated and delighted his friend Dame Ethel Smyth, and many German musicians.

Despite these frivolities, his knowledge of music was profound. He spoke of it often, and listened a great deal to musical programmes during the war. One evening, after listening to the Brahms "Requiem", he said it never seemed religious to him. He was asked whether it was the absence of the Kyrie. "No", he answered, "Brahms is just pure beauty." Later the wireless played all the old Strauss waltzes, and he said he would have liked to have written Strauss melodies more than most music, "music which had survived generation after generation of the young and the old of all nations and every phase of complicated criticism and fashion."

The late Rt. Hon. H. H. Asquith was once asked whom he considered a man of genius in his generation; he answered without a moment's hesitation: "For genius in the sense of spontaneous, dynamic intelligence, I have no doubt that I would say Maurice Baring."

Perhaps his genius consisted in his power of seeing the trend of thought and its expression in others even more quickly than they did themselves, and making it his own when he wished to; he also had great powers of abstracting his mind from things he considered valueless or unworthy in life, as in art and literature. Hence, I believe, his great reserve and detachment. He was also a very shrewd judge of men, summing them up swiftly and generally correctly—Sydney Smith's definition of an extraordinary man was applicable to him: "He has as much wit as if he had no sense, and as much sense as if he had no wit." He could in these last years of his life be as happy listening to little children talking to him or to each other, as in listening to the conversation of writers, theologians, politicians, musicians or artists.

Owing to war conditions few friends were able to reach him, and owing to ever-increasing paralysis he was unable to do more than dictate brief letters and a little verse; the latter caused him intense suffering.

Realizing that his contact with life as he had known it was over, he threw himself with zest and no expression of outward sorrow into this new existence. As its background he had the companionship of his nurse—Jean Neill—an Australian whose gaiety and understanding almost rivalled his own. She knew all that could be done to alleviate his sufferings, which was very little, but sustained him by her sunny optimism, delightful sense of humour and immense devotion. "You are not even a 'mallard imaginaire,' dear Major" she used to tell him—which was the answer the late Godfrey Webb gave on being asked what he had shot when out duck flighting. She gave him confidence and security in a martyrdom which we all realised could only be terminated by death. This was never alluded to, though Maurice wished it to be a firmly established fact; it saved him discussion about possible cures and doctors. It was also forbidden to ask after his health, and if anyone enquired whether he had slept well the answer was invariably, "That is a secret."

All those in close contact with him became his devoted slaves; amongst these was an Italian P.o.W.— Salvatore Fusi— who would listen spellbound to Maurice's perfect Italian, and helped to nurse him on his death-bed.

In his Parish Priest—Father Geddes—he found a man of wide reading and culture, who kept him constantly supplied with books and current magazines, and whose weekly visits were a great solace to him; and then, finally, and perhaps primarily, during these six years there were my children and my grandchildren; three of whom were born in the house, and the others constantly coming in and out of it.

Before dying Maurice told me this last phase of his life had been, except for the unending pain, in some ways the "richest"; largely, I think, because of the children and the family life of which he had become the loved centre. Each new-born baby was placed in his arms on its arrival, and he would say, "I think it is a *lovely* baby", looking round for ready confirmation, and asking to be allowed to hold the soft bundle of shawls "just a little longer".

Every birthday was celebrated in his bedroom, only nannies and children being admitted, for he loved the unbroken ritual of the nursery meal; the silent munching of the cousins, the "Wipe your mouth, dear"; "Only one piece at a time, Su'Rose"; "Another cup, Simon?" "May I ask you for the scones, Mrs. Tansy?" "Wipe your mouths, children, and ask Uncle Maurice if you can get down"; "Say your graces."

On asking later whether watching so long a meal had not fatigued him he would answer, it had been "perfect". No tiny incident had escaped him. Then came the feasts, Easter and Christmas, when the children surpassed themselves in making or buying him presents, all of which decorated his walls and tables until replaced by the next year's offerings. Every evening, even to two days before his death, each child was lifted in turn on to his bed and given a sweet hidden in his frail hand, which had to be blown on, or sometimes kissed, until the sweet was released. The children would then sit beside him, sleepy and contemplative, sucking their sweets; the elder ones telling him of their day's adventures, certain of his often silent attention to all they were saying, the small ones lying contentedly against his shoulders until reluctantly extracted from his bed and tucked into their own cots.

His blue budgerigar "Dempsey" was always on his bed, and talked to him constantly. He was a perpetual pleasure, and our dismay was great when his usual form of grain ceased to be imported. Mercifully, an *ersatz* blend was found in Australia and sent in time to prevent his losing weight. Dempsey's cage now hangs in the children's nursery, and he has become their "Oiseau Bleu" to be gently unravelled in their memories from him who had loved them all so much.

So spring succeeded winter for five years, and despite pain, bad news, and the death of two much loved members of his adopted family, and of many others, the resurrection of the world came to him as a perpetual miracle of beauty. The last spring of his life was unusually lovely. Watching with him the sudden green of the larches in late April, after an apparently unending winter, I quoted his own lines from "I.M."

"So when the Spring of the world shall shrive our
   stain
   After the winter of war."
he tossed them aside, "Such poor verse—look! . . ." And indeed for hours he watched the changing beauty of the world within his small compass of vision; never unconscious of it.

The wireless was an enormous boon to him, and we would not only listen to four war bulletins a day, but to all classical music and many plays; indeed our routine was arranged so as to miss nothing we liked; and how wide and varied was his taste! Little came amiss. The "Zoo man" and Mr. Middleton on Gardening were very popular, if unexpected, treats.

But when the wireless was uninteresting, by the light of candles (for we had no electricity) I would read aloud to him during our long northern nights.

23

We read and re-read Dickens, Meredith, Thackeray, Scott, Stevenson, Jane Austen, the Brontës, Trollope, Conrad and all the English classics. During the day he would read with avidity contemporary literature, and occasionally modern verse, but for the long evenings we stepped into a world where the characters were such old friends that in their well-known society there was no element of surprise, and one could find content and repose. Sometimes he would tell one what he was reading to himself. "Do you remember", he said once, looking up from a book on the R.A.F., "what one boy says to another at Eton after a game of Fives, and *has* said since Henry VI's day? 'Thank you for the game', and the other says 'Thank you for playing.' Now listen to this. The French Army, having a difficult time, was supported by the R.A.F. who bombarded the enemy from above. After the battle was over the French Army signalled, 'Merci pour le R.A.F.' The Air Force replied 'Merci pour le sport.' "

In 1941 the Canadian Forestry Corps arrived to cut down the surrounding forests. Officers and men were often in the house and warmly welcomed by Maurice, and though many at first were rather shy of so very sick a man, he soon managed to establish an easy intimacy with them, especially with their Chaplain—Captain McGuire—a great Redemptorist Missionary, who was destined to be with him when he died. He made these men forget their homesickness, and many of them turned to him for consolation and optimism in the darkest hours of the war; for at no time did he think the war was lost, though there were moments when he could not see how it could be won. My son's friends, mostly officers on leave, would be riotously entertained in his bedroom, where they would sit till early morning enchanted by his gaiety and understanding of their problems and points of view. Though these evenings tired him greatly, he would never allow them to be curtailed, and gave all his dying strength to entertaining these guests and listening to their troubles.

Naval disasters were those which affected him most deeply. For many years he had spent two or three months every spring at sea with his friend, Admiral Sir William Fisher. His long association with the Navy made the death of a ship an almost unbearable agony; but he was passionately interested in every phase of the war.

Having known and loved so many German people and towns, and much German literature, it was an interest to him when an Austrian political refugee— Dr. Stephan Zeissl—came to work as a forester in our neighbourhood, and the week-ends he spent with us helped to break the monotony of life. But who could find monotony in "life" as Maurice Baring understood it? Least of all himself, or those who surrounded him. From all angles life beat down upon him and through him; he lived with a fierce intensity and a perfect resignation at one and the same time. We followed sometimes with faltering feet, but felt with him that "Life is short, and the art long; the occasion instant, decision difficult; experiment perilous."

When the news of the liberation of Paris reached us on the wireless, a French military Chaplain, Captain de Naurois, M.C., who had served with great distinction in my son's Brigade on "D" Day, and was on sick leave at

C

the time, recited the "Te Deum", standing at the salute by Maurice's bedside.

From then onwards, despite the bitter fighting, Maurice's anxiety over the war relaxed. This great European had sung his "Nunc Dimittis". A friend said to him that she felt such peace in his room. "You have had an inner citadel ever since your illness began." He laughed and said "All I can say is, there have been some pretty fierce skirmishes outside it" (meaning the intolerable suffering there had been). "But, Maurice, it is a miracle to us all that your inner peace is never disturbed." "How could it be?", was the quiet answer. He suffered greatly, though generally in silence (for he knew the frailty and folly of human nature), from the tone of the wireless and much of the Press over our vanquished enemy. He foresaw that our attitude of mind would have to change. With the end of the summer he seemed to grow more remote from the events of this world, except those which affected his immediate surroundings; for these his sympathy and care never varied, and if possible increased. But the problem of the world's agony he felt now could only be left to its Creator.

He died on 14th December, 1945, and as a final page to this inadequate account of five and a half years filled with so much laughter and suffering, so much strength of mind and discipline of thought, I will add my diary of the last few days of his life.

11th December, 1945.

M. I want you to tell me the very funny joke you made about St. Thomas and the atomic bomb, to René last August.

L. I can't remember it. I will try to this evening—
it needs a lot of working out. I think it was rather
like this . . . .

M. Not at all, you've got it all wrong.

L. Well, it makes you laugh a lot even now, perhaps
we can't improve upon it? Could it be this . . . .?

M. No, even less, go away, you make me laugh too
much.

Later in the morning . . .

M. They lift me so badly (his back was in a very bad
state despite perfect nursing, and every movement
was agony. A new nurse had arrived that morning
who was unfamiliar with the work).

L. It will be better next time. It was probably absence
of team work.

M. Do you know what Sarasate said when he was asked
how he liked Joachim's playing?

L. No.

M. (with strong accent). I go *home* and *practice*.

That day I finished correcting the French translation
of *Passing By*. There were mistakes on every page
(I did not tell him this), but there were also some
passages translated literally which would be in-
comprehensible to the French, mainly on the position
of Anglicans. These required three difficult footnotes
which he corrected with infinite care and a good
deal of laughter. "The French must not think the
English are *always* wrong", he said. His temperature
was over 104°, but his mind was very clear whilst doing
this. He was enchanted when it was over and liked the
name "En Passant"—the print and the "Dédicace".

L. It reads so much better in French than in English.

M. Yes. You are so much more like a Frenchwoman than any one else.

L. It will have a great success.

M. (wearily) I wonder; anyway it's over—an enormous relief!

That evening the children came in as usual. He always made a great effort to be very normal with them. Fiona was lifted on to his bed and laid her golden head on his shoulder—their faces lit by candlelight—his eyes closed, hers large and watchful.

Nanny. Uncle Maurice is too tired for you to blow on his hands tonight. Neill will give you some sweets. Kiss him goodnight and come.

M. (rousing himself). Goodnight, children. Give them their sweets.

That night he was very delirious and asked me— "Are you Mary Magdalen?"

I gave him a camellia.

M. No. I see, always, *always*, always la "Dame aux Camélias".

Movement was becoming a torture, and having no second nurse, we got an ex-batman from the Lovat Scouts to help us, called Jack Fraser.

Jack. Would you like some cake and tea, sir?—you've had no lunch.

M. Yes.

When it was brought he said "Jack must open the Champagne. We will all three drink some."

L. Yes. It will do us all good.

M. You hate it—but it will do *Jack* good.

We listened that night to Beethoven's Seventh

Symphony. Maurice said, "Quite beautiful—a lovely second movement, the loveliest of all."

Later he became very restless.

L. Shall I say the Rosary?

M. Yes, in French.

L. Do you remember Ethel singing "L'Ave Maria de l'Enfant" in your room in Gray's Inn?

M. Yes. And the *silence* after she had finished it. Only the plane trees rustling in the wind through the open window. Go on—say it now—now in Latin —now Italian.

L. I don't know it in Italian.

M. Call in Salvatore. (Salvatore said it.) Now in Spanish.

L. No, no, once again in German. Then you'll sleep.

M. That's enough. Our Lady will finish it for us— Goodnight.

12*th December.*

The night had been very bad. I told him Father McGuire had arrived in England and would be with us next day.

M. Isn't that wonderful!

L. Shall we listen to Schubert's Quintet for Strings this afternoon?

M. Oh, that will be lovely—*What* a treat!

L. You don't know how lovely Fiona looked lying on your shoulder last night—like a lovely sleepy Persian cat, so warm and soft.

M. I asked Cecilia once when she was lying in her cot, warm and deliciously fat, what she was made of. She looked up without winking and said "Dust".

29

Later.

L. Who said "Querelle de Moines" about the Reformation?

M. (lightning swift)—The Pope—Leo X.

Pause.

I am so afraid if I die now that it is an inconvenient time for Rosie and Shimi—so near Christmas—the house so full—the servants so busy.

L. It is always the right moment.

M. Yes, the Right Moment always, always.

L. This afternoon I am going to rest on the sofa near you.

M. Darling—darling—what fun that will be—go away now—*What* a treat! Come back.

L. You are so tired.

M. I am *never* tired. Sit near me. It is so strange. I cannot say a prayer these days—not a single prayer.

L. So unnecessary—so many are saying your name to God—night and day.

M. Tell them to SHOUT it.

L. I will read you Charlemagne's Prayer and l'Abbé Perreyve's. He repeated after me this prayer and said "Re-read the lines:

'Ayez pitié de ceux qui s'aimaient et qui ont été séparés, de ceux qui luttent contre les difficultés, et qui ne cessent de tremper leurs lèvres dans les amertumes de la vie.'"

L. You have said it. Shall I read it again?

M. Yes.

Jack later came in to ask for orders for lunch.

M. A beef-steak and some raspberries. Would that be strengthening?

Jack. Very strengthening indeed, sir.

He could touch neither.

The Schubert Quintet was perfection.

Neill wanted to move his bed so that he could watch the sunset, but he seemed so absorbed in the music that we did not dare to disturb him.

He was very delirious that evening, but about 7 o'clock he made me say some Heine to him. I said "Die Walfahrt nach Kevlaar." I stumbled over many verses—Maurice corrected and helped me each time. Then "Mein Kind, wir waren Kinder" and "Ein Fichtenbaum."

M. Is Stephan coming? I hope he'll come soon.

L. Veronica has a new "follower".

M. A beau? How exciting—will she marry him?

L. I don't know—that is not yet known.

M. That *is* news!

It was very difficult for him to drink. He said: "There is a 'sourde guerre', but an unceasing one, between Nurse and Jack as to who can manage the 'white pail' (feeding cup) best—rather exhausting—both do it so well—neither can make me drink."

Nanny came in to help Nurse and Salvatore move him.

M. Nanny is perfect—Goodnight.

13th December.

From 6 o'clock a.m. Maurice asked with anxious patience whether Fr. McGuire had arrived.

At 11 o'clock we heard him—I said "that must be his gay footstep".

M. "Yes—always so gay—but only externally."

Father McGuire kissed Maurice—sat down and lit a cigarette—no sickroom *égards*—Maurice enchanted

31

but too exhausted to speak—or even listen. A very bad morning. In the afternoon we talked again of Veronica.

L. Do you think she will marry her beau?

M. Oh, yes. She certainly will—and they will be immensely happy.

There was no music that evening except a potpourri of old songs—I turned on the wireless at "*Plaisir d'Amour*".

M. I can't bear it.

L. Nor can I—we will turn it off.

M. Why did you turn it off? It was only unselfishness. I *insist* on hearing the end—I know you love it— Turn it on again. (Luckily it was over. Later there was some Sibelius.)

M. Too long and stodgy—very like Finland—lovely moments—Goodnight.

14*th December*.

Fr. McGuire came in for a few moments in the morning. Maurice was very ill.

M. Who is the man in the Gospel who is "sent empty away?"

L. Could it be "the rich he hath sent empty away?"

M. Yes—very probably—very probably. Read me from my prayer book the prayers of Sainte Thérèse.

L. I'll look—I don't seem able to find it.

M. First come three Russian prayers, then Charlemagne's, then Perreyve's, then a Latin one, then hers.

Later.

Neill. What would you like for lunch, dear Major?

M. Whatever you would like me to have.

At three o'clock Fr. Geddes read the Prayers for the Dying. I think Maurice heard them.

From three o'clock to eleven o'clock Fr. McGuire, Neill and I never left him. I spoke to him often—if he heard he made no sign.

At a quarter to eleven Fr. McGuire lit the candles on each side of the Crucifix at the foot of his bed, and gave him Final Absolution, and we recited the Litany for the Dying.

At eleven o'clock Maurice died.

Fr. McGuire stood up and said the Magnificat.

II

Letters

To Lady Fisher   18th November, 1898

My dearest Cecilia,

It is pitch dark from fog and I have got cramp in the middle finger of my right hand, and so I can't write as long a letter as I meant to write to you this morning when I went to bed last night. I sent you a book called *The Travellers' Tale*—at least I told Mr. Bain to send it you. Did he? I then read it, and found it was not at all a child's book, although it looked like one. In fact, that it was more suited for a stockbroker, a retired banker, or the directors of the South Western Railway. But I think it may amuse you all the same.

In a few days I shall send you a book of fairy tales, and when you have read that, and if you are very naughty indeed and make Margaret cry, and pinch Miss Weise till she calls for a policeman, and if you adopt an impertinent tone to the Headmaster, and snub the Provost, and contradict Mr. Rawlins twice, and strangle Mrs. Warre after pouring two sticks of of boiling black sealing wax down her nostrils, and say "How do you do" to Miss Copeman in Chapel, then, I will send you a surprise box!

Goodbye, or to put it more plainly as the Duchess said, never imagine yourself not to be otherwise than what it might appear to others, that what you were or

might have been was not otherwise than what you had
been would have appeared to them to be otherwise!

B. M. S.

S (that red S means that the letter has been seen by
Lord Salisbury; he said it was the sort of letter which
must be answered by shops).

How is Hubert?

Please write to me.

British Embassy, Paris
15th February, 1899

To Mrs. Cornish

My dear Mrs. Cornish,

I am sitting alone in my room; the shaded electric
light scarcely lets me see the photographs of the many
Titians and Giorgiones round on the walls. I was
longing for a letter and I go out and find one from you!
I asked for a stone and I was given a pearl.

I am in the depths of depression: rather comforted
by a little French artist who came to see me this afternoon, and said that the French jubilation over our
defeats depressed him as much as the Dreyfus calumnies;
although he was against the war. And that he thought
the courage of the English soldier was sublime—
like that of the Cadets de Gascogne—"qui sont ces
gens qui se font tous tuer". They are the sons of the
Dartmoor Hills, of Plymouth Sound and Lynmouth
Hills. Next Thursday I am going to see Anatole
France. . . .

My dear Mrs. Cornish,

I have never thanked you for your most charming letter. The most spoiling letter I have ever had in my life. I miss Eton dreadfully. But this place is immensely interesting and exhilarating. I had influenza badly the night before last; but there is something so recuperative in the atmosphere that I am about, and practically well today. No wonder the French people bound up again from their disasters like giants refreshed, rejoicing to soar and sing in the "ne plus ultra"—as the Headmaster would say. President Faure's funeral was a most beautiful pageant, starting at eleven in the morning; Paris was bathed in light and mist "all bright and glittering in the smokeless air".

The town looked as if it had just been made—"When *Paris* like a mist rose into towers", and every now and then you heard fragments of very soft military music and a low mumbling of drums the whole time, and an intermittent booming of minute guns.

I walked behind four huge Germans: the four biggest men in Germany, whom the German Emperor, with that extraordinary delicate tact which he possesses, sent to remind the French of certain unpleasant facts. The Service in Notre Dame was most magnificent: one organ answering the other: the most perfect orchestra and singing.

I don't know if you still take any interest in the Dreyfus case. I fancy (although there is such a lull just at present that you would think that no such case had ever existed) that when the Cour de Cassation gives its decision there will be the most tremendous outburst—that is, if it is in favour of Dreyfus, as nine people out of ten have never for one instant taken that eventuality as belief in the infallibility of Courts Martial.

The infallibility of the Pope is a difficult doctrine for some people; but the infallibility of seven officers! Good gracious! I won't bore you any more.

27th March, 1899

To Mrs. Cornish

I am having such fun here now. I went to the première of Hamlet the other night with Betty Montgomery: you must be sure and see it: it is the ultimate triumph of *intelligence:* the victory of intelligence over every obstacle on "la matière". Sarah attempted the impossible and achieved it with ease.

I am reading Ruskin and *Les Evangiles* by Renan in my spare moments.

1st November, 1899

To Mrs. Cornish

I am going again to Tristan tonight: the orchestra (Lamoureux) is wonderful—it is like a forest of wood notes and a magic sea mixed. The singers are execrable; however, they didn't attempt to sing so it didn't much matter.

37

I came back from Courances on Wednesday evening, the day of ill news (the Fall of Ladysmith); "they brought me bitter news to read, and bitter tears to shed." The unkindest thing was I travelled up from Courances with a French officer, a violent nationalist; as we got into the train my eye caught the heading of defeat in the newspapers which I had bought at the station, so I stuffed them in my pocket and talked without drawing breath about musical chairs and Shakespeare, till we arrived at Paris.

But the French individuals—though they are very disapproving of the war—Dreyfusards to a man—are full of admiration for our soldiers, and are nice about it. Generals Negrier and Roget say that Gen. White was perfectly correct in what he did, and that they would have done the same.

Courances is a red brick Henry IV château surrounded by a great piece of water which makes a noise. It is in the middle of a Louis XVI park with shapely alleys, avenues, canals and ponds, and inhabited by exiled peacocks and discredited white pheasants; also by a tiny dog—a square inch big—called Hercules. The trees were like fire when I was there; golden torches—for the funeral of the year. "Es mögen", I thought, "die letzten Küsse des scheidenden Sommers sein."

We drive to Fontainebleau both afternoons through the dying forest which, like Mary Queen of Scots, had put on its most splendid clothes to die, and we visited the Château which looked more beautiful and more completedly sad than anything I have ever seen.

The dinners were very amusing. I never heard so much talk in my life. We discussed Wagner, and whether the greatest art needed people to be educated in order to appreciate it, at the top of our voices, and I suddenly became conscious that I was insulting an academician. The next night the academician came to dinner with me, and welcomed the opportunity in order to talk about the Affaire Dreyfus which he had been longing to do, and so we plunged once more into that luring whirlpool, and I came out an uncompromising anti-Dreyfusard, which I have long suspected that I was.

The next night we discussed Napoleon's character till we were hoarse.

7th February, 1900

To Mrs. Cornish

Today after weeks of rain the glorious sun uprist and bathed Paris in dazzling whiteness. I went for a long walk on the quays and bought a *History of the Vandals* and a Racine—25 cents each. I had an hour's conversation with my bookbinder as he worked on a stool at a most elaborate bit of mosaic work; inlaying tiny bits of crimson Morocco in gold fleurs-de-lis, while his wife from the next room threw in desultory remarks.

We talked about millionaires and their ignorance, and about bibliophiles and their angelic sweetness, and about big books and small books and vellum linings and ciseléd leaves. People were working all round and at the end Mercier's wife ran and fetched the Mass book her husband had bound for her wedding; such an elaborate binding has never been seen. It had every

39

flower in the Garden of Eden and every colour in the rainbow, and every device of heraldry; it was a bit of sheer bravura: like Melba's roulades in Lucia or like Sarasate when he plays Au Clair de la Lune, if he ever does.

Hilaire Belloc was here on Sunday. We went to the Louvre and to the Concert Rouge, and to Vespers at St. Sulpice, and to Benediction at Notre Dame, and then for a long drive on the top of an omnibus, during which Hilaire pointed out to me Danton's house, and Danton's prison, and Danton's café, and Danton's chapel, and Danton's tennis court, and Danton's "Kegelbahn", and Danton's tobacconist.

What a wonderful book the *Mill on the Floss* is! How intensely poetical—the epic of childhood, with its mystery and awe and moments of misery. I think she knew Stephen Guest was what he was.

22nd February, 1900

To Mrs. Cornish

I went to see Anatole France this morning. There was an extraordinary collection of people—ex-Governors of Colonies, and young students with beards and big ties. One of them was a very young and very violent anti-militarist. He said the Boer War was a crime just as the French expedition to Madagascar had been; and any army was a criminal thing. I told him that I thought wars and armies were necessary evils, and inevitable if painful results of human nature. At the end of the conversation he said: "Je vous

demande pardon de la brutalité de mes sentiments."
I said, "Pas du tout, Monsieur. Je vous demande
pardon de la douceur des miens."

Anatole France's house is like a bit of the Middle
Ages with old doors, knockers, and high stiff chairs.

The news seems better, doesn't it, but one scarcely
dares be pleased.

Goodbye,

Yours,

M.B.

17th March, 1900

To Mrs. Cornish

I must write you a line about the first night of
L'Aiglon to which I went.

The theatre was paved with beaten celebrities.
The Dreyfusard sat next to the Anti-Dreyfusard, the
Jew next to the Nationalist. The dress circle glittered
with intelligent eyes, and the boxes were elegant with
stupid beauty and consummate rogues.

Sarah's entrée was glorious. It was difficult to believe
she wasn't Napoleon's son. She looked 17, fresh,
young, slight and manly, and soon the electricity of her
personality got the audience into a state of delirium.

All the epic of Napoleon was in her eyes. The play
is I think, very fine, an épopée; more human than
Cyrano, and on a higher level altogether, though less
finished, compact and coherent. The verses the same
type, but I think more serious.

Better, of course, as in Cyrano, to hear than to read.

Life seemed to fade the next day—after this bit of

history which was like a looking-glass to a larger history.

I forgot to say that in the entracte of *L'Aiglon* I went and kissed Sarah's hand. In her loge were Sardou, Anatole France, Duc de Rohan, Reinach, Hervieu, Coquelin and many others!

23rd March, 1900

To Mrs. Cornish

Yesterday morning I went to see Anatole France again in his high mediæval cell. Jaurès, the Socialist, was there talking with a rich flow of language and a Gascon accent, and in the corner observing the cobwebs was M. Emile Zola. Anatole France didn't like *L'Aiglon*. Unfortunately it has been made a political question, and as the Anti-Dreyfusards have adopted it, the Dreyfusards feel obliged—and are convinced as they say so—to say that it is worthless. Suddenly, however, he put Æschylus on the block and talked for half an hour in the most brilliant and subtle way about this author, who is happily out of reach of the Dreyfus affair. I, for one, was intoxicated by *L'Aiglon*, be it good or bad: I think there is room in the music of the world for the band of brass instruments and fifes and drums skilfully playing inspiring martial themes, as well as for the Schumann quintet and the Kreutzer Sonata.

Rostand has got by instinct what Ibsen learned after being a stage manager for many years, and what Shakespeare as an actor must have known and realised— the "doigté du dramaturge", an incomparable instinct for stage effect and appreciation of the value of the footlights. And what to me is his greatest charm is that he is a poet who has deliberately taken a poetical view of existence and woven his dreams, and built up fabrics of fantasy, and blown enchanted soap bubbles for the joy of it; he has no mission, no purpose; he brings no "pageant of a bleeding heart"; he does not seek the cosmic significance of modern life including the telephone; nor has he come as a physician to probe the wounds of his generation; but every now then in the cycle of humanity it is necessary that an irresponsible singer should come and say in spite of much opposition that there are many beautiful things in the world, and that it is good that someone should retell the old story which it is not thought worth while to repeat—the old story of Spring and Summer, of Hero and Leander, of Romeo and Juliet, of Captains like D'Artagnan, Kings like Henry V, Emperors like Napoleon, Knights like Bayard, soldiers like Ney and Lannes, Queens like Cleopatra and Marie Antoinette, and sing the losing side, chant a golden optimism in spite of evidences and appearances to the contrary, fight for impossible causes and resuscitate faded romances. This Rostand has done, and whatever may be the merit of his poetry, his lines have often the smell of spring flowers, and often the sound of pipes and bells or golden harps. Dieu Merci.

Friday, June 1900

To Mrs. Cornish

And I may come on Sunday after all.
And in the Cloisters I shall ask for lunch.

43

And I shall smoke a Russian cigarette
On Fellows Eyot. Miss Copeman will be there
Puffing and blowing in a violet blouse,
And asking with enquiring startled eyes
Whether red roses might mean Martyrdom,
And I must hurry off at half-past four
Returning on the Monday. Should this suit
And be to all concerned convenient.

And in the rocking turret I shall sleep.

Copenhagen
10th August, 1900

To Hubert Cornish, Esq.

My dear Hubertine,

It is imperative that you should write to me
immediately. This is a Hildesheim. I feel I ought to be
at the Timme's; Les Moeurs Danoises are very simple;
the King of Denmark meets one at the station and
carries your luggage on his back to the Hotel.

I had a very wonderful journey here, but I was
horribly disturbed on the steamer by a Dane in an
Alpaca ulster and spectacles, shooting a stuffed wild
duck in the cabin next to mine all night. When I
arrived the British Fleet were sailing up the Sound and
bombarding the capital, which was tumbling to pieces
like a child's brick castle.

It is dark and raining, and the climate makes one feel
as if one had no bones at all, and makes one's nerves
sing so that you feel like Nietzsche and Hedda Gabler
mixed; but after a day I believe you feel gloriously
well and wake up as Hereward the Wake.

I am going to take two delicious rooms with a stove and a sofa, and a spare room for you to come and stay in; you must. I have already read more in the last day and a half than in the last two years. I miss you all very much, but I feel as if I was in Heaven, and that it was useless to indulge in "de vains regrets"—Il faut beaucoup aimer le Danemark is my new motto— and "beau comme un Danois" is my new phrase.

I don't think it is at all dank, but then there are no dank places except Scotland and the Isle of Man and South Africa. You will come here, won't you?

I have been reading a book by Maupassant and knocked down by his extraordinary mastery of his art and his tools—but here I stop on the verge of an—?

Sincerely,

M. B.

Sosnofka,

To Vernon Lee (Miss Paget)   14th *October,* 1903

... I think that the existence of merely frivolous people who are bent on amusement is a necessary element in this grey world, and that Helen of Troy, Mary Stuart, Ninon de l'Enclos, Diane de Poitiers, Petronius Arbiter, and Charles II are equally necessary in the scheme of things as St. Paul, Thomas Aquinas, Marcus Aurelius, John Knox, Pym and Lady Jane Grey, whom we appreciate all the more by reason of contrast.

Again I think there is a great deal of injustice inspired often by envy which it is irritating to contemplate,

45

against what is contemptuously called "les gens du monde", who, besides having given us our most remarkable statesmen and rulers, have also produced Catullus, Dante, Bacon, Montaigne, Ronsard, Sir Philip Sidney, Shelley, Pushkin, Tolstoi, and Tourgeneff. Their frivolity, their selfishness, their extravagance are always spoken of; their qualities are taken for granted and the charm of their qualities were matters of course to themselves; things they did naturally and thought no more of than of being decently clothed. These qualities have a great attraction when they are tested in the crucible of tragic events, such as the French Revolution, and they produce the gold of heroism. Heroism too of, to me, a particularly attractive kind, "the unselfishness of the selfish", "the unworldliness of the worldly", suddenly manifest without fuss, cant or pretension. I like the account of Biron's death in the French Revolution, I like the manifestation of that kernel of unflinching and un-compromising instinct, which, blent with the utmost cynicism and irony, has caused men in various epochs to go laughingly to death for a cause or a creed in which they did not believe. Again I have personally noted this, that the idle frivolous class regard the other laborious one with respect and accept their censure with indifference; whereas the laborious often regard the frivolous with outward contempt mingled with an inward gnawing and hankering envy. We know the frequent combination of the socialist and the snob.

Do not misunderstand me or think I am either blind to what is hollow and sham in "social" (hateful word) life, or to what is great and noble in the lives of those

46

who renounce it and all its works. All I say is that tolerance is necessary on both sides; the frivolous have qualities and the strenuous and sober have faults which should suffice to prevent them from continually seeking for the motes in the eyes of others.

Personally the opinion I most respect, and most care for, is that of those who are neither specialists nor workers, who live away from cliques and côteries and have no other motive than the desire of expressing their likes and dislikes, and I think if they are intelligent their criticism is the best which is to be got.

Forgive this long harangue.

Yours,

M. B.

British Embassy, St. Petersburg
4th August, 1905

To Vernon Lee (Miss Paget)

The impression one receives from the Greek Church in a Russian village or in the Cathedral of the Assumption, or at Moscow, is totally different from what you describe as happening at Venice.

At Moscow one is struck by the extraordinary mixture of devoutness and practicalness, a kind of pagan quality in the worship utterly devoid of self-consciousness, and being performed in the manner in which these things must be done, because they have always been done like that.

The Church is crowded to begin with; every class— peasants, children, women, soldiers, generals, officials —all standing up in a crowd and every single person carrying on his particular devotions separately. For instance one man remains stolidly immovable when certain saints are mentioned, but prostrates himself at the names of others; he worships his particular favourite saint more than others.

Then sometimes quite suddenly a peasant will give way to an excess of devotion and prostrate himself nine times running. And all the time the magnificent bass singing is going on.

Yours,

M. B.

3, *Gray's Inn Place, High Holborn*
9th June, 1905
To *Vernon Lee (Miss Paget)*

. . . Goethe's best lyrics seem to me no better than Shelley's. Shelley's *The World's Great Age, I Arise from Dreams of Thee* and *Swiftly Walk o'er the Western Wave* seem to me unapproachable and unique. Goethe's also; but they seem to me two different things; not the same in kind; like comparing a butterfly's wing with a rose leaf. . . .

M. B.

10th October, 1906
To *Vernon Lee (Miss Paget)*

. . . I was interested in what you say about Bayreuth. I agree absolutely. So far as Bayreuth itself goes the only enjoyment to me is the orchestra, which, when I heard it, I thought divine; and better than any other I had heard. As to Wagner, I agree with all you say; yes, d'Annunzio has the same, exactly the same, quality of slowness and hypnotic mesmerism; also I think the gift of doing something to language which introduces another element into it, just as Wagner does with sound. At its worst it is like the noise people make by rubbing the rim of a glass of water; at its best it is something very mysteriously beautiful; and then, attack it as one may, the fact of the genius and the bigness of scale remains and the peculiar things Wagner has said which no one else has. What I like best of all is the Meistersinger. As for Parsifal, I abhor it. It is a grotesque parody of the Mass with conjuring tricks, and Oh! the length!

Another artist who seems to me in this category is Swinburne. Almost every poem of Swinburne's is too long; not because it is too long in actual size and length, but because everything that is said lasts too long, the tempo is too much drawn out. Take one of his finest poems, the *Elegy on Baudelaire*. It misses being quite magnificent because every stanza is too long, whereas the whole poem might have been twice as long and yet not too long had Catullus written it for instance. That is why I think Racine is such a great poet; he is as perfect a master over his means as Mozart, and gives you a thousand lights and shades.

M. B.

British Consulate, Moscow
To Hilaire Belloc   20th March, 1906

My Dear Hilaire,

Thank you for your letter which came like a ray of sunlight to a gloomy land and filled me with dance and

Provençal song and sunburnt birth. The phrase is Keats'. Had I someone to whom I could dictate, I would write longer and fuller letters. As is it I have to push a heavy pen over slippery paper with feeble fingers and uncertain aim. . . .

To go on now to really important matters. The verse you quote in your letter is admirable. I think your verse is as good as Pope's and that you might write a poem like the "Rape of the Lock" half satirical with passages of real beauty in it. I wish you would do so.

When is your verse coming out? I see you often ask questions in the House. The next time you make a speech send me the report of it in case I should miss it.

I have just come back from plains of melting snow over which the larks were singing. The streams were in flood and turned meadows into lakes in which the willow trees floated like pale shadows.

I am till Death and perhaps beyond,

Yours,

M.B.

To Hilaire Belloc

Moscow
21st March, 1906

My Dear Hilaire,

I congratulate you on your speech on Beer. I agreed with every word of it.

Please let me know to the following direction
what your prospects are.

Sosonofka,Morshansk,Tambov. via Moscow
This is the direction.Please write me a long
letter. I am yours

Maurice

This letter is not well type-written—But then, you know, it is the pen and not the typewriter which is mightier than the sword.

St. Petersburg
No date.

To Hilaire Belloc

My Dear Hilaire,
I have answered your last delightful letter through Constantine Benckendorff, the son of the Ambassador, who has just gone to London and asked me to give him a letter of introduction to you—he is a great admirer of your prose and verse. So I have done so. Please be kind to him. He was in the Navy; through all Port Arthur and then a prisoner. . . .

This was the letter of introduction.

Moscow, British Consulate
28th April
11th May, 1906

To Hilaire Belloc

My Dear Hilaire, I have received your letter,
Written in verse, which scarcely could be better;
I have not your facility; though I
By writing prose to win my bread feel dry
And void of all expressive force. I mean
My prose is jejune, barren, dry and lean.

51

But then my verse is every bit as bad;
My hand is weary and my soul is sad.
Inspite of which I lose no time, you see,
To answer your epistle tunefully.
The bearer of this letter; which is not
A simple rigmarole of senseless rot;
But has a purpose, which I will explain,
This double relative will cause you pain—
The bearer of this letter, I repeat,
Is Benckendorff once of the Russian Fleet
And still connected with the Russian Navy.
He narrowly escaped the home of Davy
Jones; I mean the locker, that's the word
Which sailors use, when sailors, so I've heard,
Seek suddenly the bottom of the sea;
Well Benckendorff has just applied to me
With the request that I should be so kind
To bring about, that is if you don't mind,
A meeting between him and you; his wish
Is to make your acquaintance. Old fried fish
Is what he likes to eat; this is a lie
But, Hilaire, you're aware as well as I
That when one writes in verse, the final rhyme
Is all important, there is seldom time
To turn one's phrase until truth coincides
With metre, not in bronze I write but dust
And therefore say not what I wish, but must.
Well, Benckendorff, the eldest son of him
You know, (who wears a hat without a brim),
The brother of his sister whom you met
One night at Mrs. Horner's (it was wet)
And once again in some obscure Hotel,

Where palm-trees grow just as they do in Hell,
The son too of his mother, whom you know,
Admires your prose and verse; while to and fro
He paced the hatches of the "Retirzan"
He used to spout your verse on Yucatan.
He wishes much to meet you, so I send
This note through him to you, to recommend
Him.   Show him London's sights:—the House of Lords
One day when you will strike the quivering chords,
In the responsive breasts of fellow-men;
I mean, of course, the House of Commons.   Then
Show him Gambrinus, where the chucker out
So very rudely bandied us about.
Take him to Brice's where a man of sense
Can dine (including wine) for eighteen pence.
Show him the little haunts where we so oft
Have drunk port wine until our brains grew soft.
Show him the Cafe Royal and Mont Blanc
And little Alphonse and the "Cœur de Sang"
(There's no such place but rhyme not sense dictates)
I mean the place where waiters wash the plates
With their own pocket handkerchiefs.   Goodbye;
Dear Hilaire; for my stylograph runs dry;
So does my verse, my prose; and all I've got
To say is this: (the rest is mainly rot).
This is to introduce a friend of mine
To you (his Man of War once struck a mine)
(The rhyme is rich but useless) if you're kind
To him; both he and I will thankful be.
I am your most devoted friend.
                              M.B.

To Hilaire Belloc

Thanks for letter; there was not a cent
To pay because the post here are content
With twopence and too lazy to apply
For surtax of an extra halfpenny.
Have you made Benckendorff's acquaintance yet
And got my letter?   Hilaire, don't forget,
This, and that I expect to hear from you
In prose or verse. I have not any rue
To send you; but I send my love instead:
Good night, for it is time to go to bed.

M.B.

To Hilaire Belloc

My Dear H,

Oddly enough I haven't got a copy of the Sonnet.
I never wrote out a fair copy except on your book. I
wrote the Sonnet on an envelope in a music hall where I
had to wait for an hour for someone *tanquam te apud
regalem cafem expectassem.* I send you the envelope and
an attempt at reconstruction but I don't think it a
good sonnet or worth bothering about.

Do you really think my sonnets are good? I wonder.
I was fearfully snubbed the other day for publishing a
book of verse at all by a high English official—he said
it was ridiculous. He hadn't read it and didn't mean
to; but he said this before fifteen people after dinner and
they all laughed and I felt a bloody fool. In France

nobody thinks it odd if you write verse, or here either—
they talk about it naturally; and in England it was so
until the reign of Charles II and even later I suppose, and
then the damned Puritans cast their stinking tarpaulin
of respectability over their filthy vices and pretended to
be virtuous. They will surely be damned. Bless you
Hilaire and thank you for your Sonnet which has more
strength and dignity than anything I ever wrote.

Yrs. M.B.

to H.B.

I too have travelled in the unknown land
And anchored by the unfrequented shore;
I too have heard the Stygian waters roar
And seen the foam of Lethe kiss the sand.
I too have trampled the enchanted grass
And seen the phantom hunters gallop by
And heard the ghostly bugle and the sigh
Of banished Gods that in the woodways pass.
And as a traveller brings his spoil to him
More richly graced in might and bravery
So do I give to you these records dim
Of bright adventures in the realms forlorn:
To you who heard the blast of Roland's horn
And saw Iseult set sail for Brittany

St. Petersburg

To Hilaire Belloc   No date

Dear Hilaire,

Here is a review of Yeats. I am not going to write
on the other book you sent.

1. It is historical,
2. v. long,
3. written in Hindoo English, Baboo Chinesie English which I don't understand and I told you I wouldn't review a *long* book, unless it's by Shakespeare or by you.

Yrs. M.B.

24th March and 6th April, 1907

To Hubert Cornish, Esq.

My body, dear Hubert, has fallen to pieces. *It can't do without fourteen hours sleep.* If I don't go to bed at nine and get up at eleven, I feel a wreck. This phase has succeeded a former one during which I couldn't get to sleep till four, however early I went to bed. My brain on the other hand has likewise dwindled to a husk. It can't stand anything stronger than Max Pemberton's novels, and once a week a little Rider Haggard. I read a sonnet of Shakespeare's last week, and was very ill afterwards. All this comes of having been bitten by a mad dog and "put in the hands" of Pasteur, whose injections have numbed me, body and soul.

It is very lamentable, but let's talk about Florence which is I know the coldest place in the world. I couldn't face it now after being saturated with the delicious warmth of St. Petersburg; but there comes a month in Florence when the goddess Persephone walks abroad. Sometimes it happens in March; sometimes in

April, sometimes in May, and it must be remembered that the adjoining months in which this doesn't happen are either freezing bitter with a wind that makes one cry out in physical pain, or they are a grey deluge of thin laborious rain. But when she comes, the wild tulips wave their heads over the brown furrows, and the dome of the cathedral floats like a petal in the distance; and the intolerable azure of the sky drowns and deafens and stuns one, and the lizard comes out to listen to the footfall of Persephone.

It's best not to go to Florence till the Judas tree is in flower. . . .

                    Yours,
                    M. B.

                              B.E.F. France
To Dame Ethel Smyth   25th October, 1914

. . . When the troops arrived, singing "It's a long, long way to Tipperary" at Maubeuge, after forced marches in the dark, it was one of the most tremendous moments I have ever experienced. *The most tremendous.* They swung up—or the tune swung them up—a very steep hill over the singing pavement, and the French came out and threw them flowers, fruit and cigarettes, and they looked so young, so elastic, and so invincibly cheerful, so unmixedly English, so tired and so fresh. And the thought of these men swinging on into horror undreamt of—the whole German Army—came to me like the stab of a sword, and I had to go and hide in a shop for the people not to see the tears rolling down my cheeks. I couldn't let my mind dwell on it for

E   57

days after without the gulp in my throat coming back.

I went to Mass this morning and it was nice to think I was listening to the same words said in the same way with the same gestures, that Henry V and his "contemptible little army" heard before and after Agincourt, and I stood between a man in khaki and a French Poilu and history flashed past like a jewelled dream.

M. B.

B.E.F. France

To Dame Ethel Smyth 16th June, 1916

. . . The last two times I went through Germany I didn't dare go to Hildesheim and see the Timmes, as I thought the catastrophe so near that it might come at any moment although I didn't see how it could come. I believed in the thunder clouds which I didn't see—and I felt I could not go or talk there. . . .

France

To Dame Ethel Smyth 20th September, 1916

. . . Life is a strain now, isn't it? Scaffolding falls about one daily, one's old friends and one's new friends are killed or disappear like flies; the floor of life seems to have gone, and one seems to live in a permanent eclipse and a *seasonless* world—a world with no summer and no winter, only a long, grey, neutral-tinted *Limbo*.

Raymond Asquith is the latest. I was certain he would be killed. I dined with him the night before he went back to his regiment after a spell at G.H.Q.— I felt I would never see him again. I think he deserved his glorious fate, and deserved it doubly or trebly for not being a soldier* and by having so much to give; one can't say more. . . .

He was the wittiest man I have ever known; his wit was like a shining icicle, and it was the wit that receives as well as the wit that gives. . . .

	France
To Dame Ethel Smyth	*8th October,* 1916

I have just seen in *The Times* that Mrs. Cornish's second boy Gerald was killed the other day.

He was a very loveable person and I admired him immensely. Once he went to a meeting which was strongly anti-suffragist. I don't know what the meeting was about, but he knew its temper and he yelled "Votes for Women" at the top of his voice. He was a deeply convinced suffragist and he was lashed but not very badly hurt.

He knew this was going to happen and was quite white before. I think this is one of the bravest things you can do. . . .

	*White's Club, London, S.W.*1
To M. André Maurois	*Le* 16 *mai,* 1917

Comme orateur j'ai toujours entendu dire qu'il n'y avait pas de comparaison entre Gladstone et Beaconsfield.

Gladstone a su même présenter le Budget comme

*Raymond Asquith was the eldest son of the Prime Minister, the Rt. Hon. H. H. Asquith, and a distinguished Barrister.

une féerie. Et même en conversation Gladstone n'était jamais ennuyeux.

Dizzy n'a jamais appris l'Anglais malgré ses phrases, ses épigrammes, et ses mots.

"Endymion" fourmille de *fautes d'Anglais* et des fautes qui choquent—des fausses notes.

Gladstone aussi vous direz écrivait fort mal; certes, mais ce n'était pas un écrivain, c'est parce qu'il écrivait si mal qu'il parlait si bien; ou plutôt c'est parce qu'il parlait si bien que ses discours sont ternes à lire.

C'étaient deux géants, mais non pas un géant et un *faux* géant.

M. B.

Pour une nouvelle édition.

Dizzy n'a jamais causé avec *Lord Cromer*. Il a causé avec Sir Evelyn Baring qui est *devenu* Lord Cromer longtemps après la mort de D.

Beaufort Castle

To Dame Ethel Smyth   *2nd September,* 1922

. . . Mrs. Cornish died at the beginning of August. She had a short illness—it only lasted about a fortnight. During the first week of it she continued to be passionately interested in "Middlemarch"; and then, when she realised that she was dying, she became still more passionately absorbed in what is beyond life: a happy life shot with sorrow and tragedies but rich in "vast consolations" ("I have poured into them vast consolations"; Thomas à Kempis III. 58).

Yours,
M. B.

To Dame Ethel Smyth

Beaufort Castle
6th September, 1922

. . . after many wet weeks the summer has suddenly arrived and the night before last was a *feenhaft** night: light although dark, the air intoxicating with aromatic clouds from the high lime trees, and the feeling of magic abroad, sounds of dancing coming from the distance, stamping, rhythmic shouts and the music of pipes that seemed close enough to touch and as far away as fairyland. . . .

28th November, 1923
To L. L.

In all the lovely things in music I know nothing better than the unexpectedness of the phrase "Tu es lasse, et ta danse m'attend incertaine—" the sense of the return of a friend who far away suddenly opens the door and walks in—it seems though so unexpected, so natural.

In *The Lady of the Sea* when the sailor arrives whom Duse believes to be at the end of the world—and by whom she has always been haunted, she says "Ecco-ti" in such a way that despite everything his wholly "impossible" arrival becomes what she had been awaiting —expecting . . . the divine unexpected long-expected surprise. . . .

29th July, 1925

To Dame Ethel Smyth

Some weeks ago I went to a prize fight at the Albert Hall. How refreshing to see the British public face to

*Fairylike.

face with an *art* (an *art*, mind you), and possible genius that they *liked* and *understood*.

There was the same warm, tense, embracing silence, the same unchokable outburst of applause, face to face with a clever piece of footwork, an inspired punch, a subtle feint, a faultless piece of timing, as you find in a French theatre when an actor of genius is speaking Racine, or in a German concert hall, where a violinist in a quartet is phrasing as if the composer were whispering in his ear.

Yours,

M.

Note by Dame Ethel Smyth

Laura—may I publish this?

In 1924 Maurice's activities were unknown to me, for he was staying with Lady Lovat in Scotland.

She does not profess to be good at machinery, but began learning, in that year, to drive a car, and with great difficulty had obtained a driving licence dated 5th August, 1924—5th August, 1925.

She left it two minutes in her writing table, and coming back found in the space left for "Endorsements and collisions if any":—

August 1st —Collision with train
,,　　2nd—　　　,,　　,,　　motor cycle
,,　　3rd—　　　,,　　,,　　donkey cart
,,　　4th—　　　,,　　,,　　perambulator
,,　　5th—　　　,,　　,,　　goods train
,,　　6th—Licence withdrawn.

And with infinite trouble, and after paying a heavy

fine, Lady Lovat procured a second licence which ran from 9th August, 1924—9th August, 1925. But, again, her guest got hold of it, and the incriminating space was thus filled up:—

August 27th—Collision with bicycle
  ,,   28th—   ,,   ,,   hand tricycle
  ,,   29th—   ,,   ,,   motor scooter
  ,,   30th—   ,,   ,,   charabanc
  ,,   31st —   ,,   ,,   go-cart
Sept.   1st —Licence withdrawn.

Always yours,
Ethel.

3 Gray's Inn Square, W.C.1

To Doctor Edith Somerville   12th *November, 1924*

My dear Edith,

Thank you very much for your letter. It was, I may tell you, wholesomely corrected by a review which was sent me by an organ called *The Catholic Truth Review* which said it was incredible I could have published such a book* as it was an example of the most slipshod and slovenly journalism which one could find, and an awful warning and example to writers. They said if Edwin Lear were not dead my article about him would have killed him. So there. I have every now and then a word or two from Ethel Smyth. We have both been ill, and I have been inoculated, which makes me very peevish. Never be inoculated for anything—that is the first rule in life. I break it once every six months.

Yours ever,
M. B.

Punch & Judy.

To R. Hart Davies, Esq.   29th March, 1925
c/o Heinemann & Co.

My dear Mr. Rupert, H. D.,

Your letter arrived this morning and gave me
untold delight. It is a great thing to get praise from the
young. The most precious and rare of all presents.
However undeserved (forgive my typing—it means
well).

You know that George Meredith said that though
stolen fruit was sweet, undeserved rewards are the real
stuff. That's the stuff to receive. I so agree. Your
letter to me is all the more appreciated because you
must remember that for thirty years I found it difficult
to get a book published; I mean every fresh book, as I
wrote on different subjects, was refused by the last
publisher, every single book of mine (forgive all this
egoism), until *Puppet Show of Memories* which went to
at least five publishers, and *C* which went to three,
and then Cassell said he would publish it if I cut out
the first six chapters. And I said, no, I wouldn't,
but I would boil them down into one, but they were
still adamant and said, "Pas une virgule" must remain,
and I was staying with an old lady whom I knew was
very wise, who said to me, "Don't insist", and I refused
Cassell and sent it to Heinemann who took it; and that
is the history of that. . . .

Oh dear.

I will send you as soon as it comes out my *Collected
Poems* to be published by Heinemann.

64

Thank you with all my heart; your letter gave me real *joy*.

Goodbye and thank you.

Yours,

Maurice Baring.

PS.   Swinburne answered one of C's letters and Watts Dunton never posted it, and it was found after S. died, and stolen.

3, *Gray's Inn Place, W.C.*1

To M. T. Tatham, Esq.   10th *June,* 1929

Dear Tham,

> I myself tap the keys
> And dispense with dictation.
> With incredible ease
> I myself tap the keys.
> My q's and my p's
> Sometimes need explanation.
> I myself tap the keys
> And dispense with dictation.

> I used a machine,
> In the year ninety-nine.
> When Victoria was Queen,
> I used a machine.
> I learnt "off" a Dean
> On the banks of the Tyne.
> I used a machine,
> In the year ninety-nine.

If I type fast or slow
I don't seem to type better.
I really don't know
If I type fast or slow.
Do you think Ikey Mo
Could have typed the word, Quetta?
If I type fast or slow
I don't seem to type better.

18, *Cheyne Row, Chelsea, S.W.*3

To Peter Stucley, Esq.,   17th *October,* 1930
Magdalen College

Dear Mr. Stucley,

Very many thanks for the letter in which you tell
me you are going to do me a great honour.* I am
greatly pleased and flattered. There have been interesting articles on some of my books in the past by
Chesterton, Edmund Gosse, Desmond McCarthy in
England. In Germany by Hermann Bahr in newspapers,
and in his printed journals: and in France in Charles
du Bos' *Un Journal*, in the Nouvelle Revue Française,
reprinted in Volume 4 of *Approximations* by André
Maurois (French preface to Daphne Adeane).

Now, as to how to get at them. My sister, Lady
Reid, has a book in which there are a good many
cuttings of this kind, and I have a book at the binders
which contains about a dozen interesting foreign
articles by Bahr, Gabriel Marcel, Mainsard and
Anglaret. I could send you the latter as soon as it
comes from the binder. Return it at your leisure, but

*Mr. Stucley was compiling an article on M.B.'s Reviews.

if this is too irksome, and it is in no light sense that I say this, *throw it on to the fire* (it would have to be a bonfire).

Yours sincerely,
Maurice Baring.

An example of Maurice's typing

Half-Way House, Steyning Road, Rottingdean
11th November, 1933

To Lady Rosebery
    (as typed when collecting for a Musician's Fund)

Dear Eva,
    i enclose a cheque from St. John Hutchinson.
I was wondering whether there was anyth ng one could do to spurtye female conscience.
Byt ass you say bookmakers are the only genreous patrons of the arts nd the intellect of music and literarture.
I have always know thi all my life.
i emain you obedoent serbvant
Maurice Baring

Half-Way House, Steyning Road, Rottingdean
16th December, 1936

To Sir Ronald Storrs

My dear Ronald,
    Alas! too late to make any further corrections. A second edition has already been printed, leaving in a

misquotation of Milton—-"noble minds" for "noble mind"—pardonable, because "noble minds" is the translation of the Latin (Tacitus). It was due to the pedantry of the University Press that the first words of that line were left out. They left them out because they didn't occur in the translation, missing, as you rightly point out, the whole point. I have got the Kruppential Shakespeare, and I have read his books on Hamlet and his text. I think the book called *What happens in Hamlet* is a thrilling book. The test, too, is absorbing. *The Diary of Master William Silence* I think you would enjoy.

Thank you so much for sending the Italian books. I am so glad that Krupp was Essen-tially kind.

Yours always,

M. B.

*Half-Way House, Steyning Road, Rottingdean
le 16 novembre, 1937*

To Monsieur l'Abbé Mugnier de Nôtre Dame, Paris.

Cher Monsieur l'Abbé,

Je ne peux pas vous dire combien j'ai été enchanté d'avoir de vos nouvelles. Je passe presque tout mon temps couché. Cela me fatigue de rester assis sur une chaise plus d'une demie heure. Je ne suis guère beaucoup plus heureux couché, car aussitôt couché, je commence à trembler. Ma maladie, paralysie agitans, est très difficile à contrecarrer, mais tout de même je vois beaucoup de monde. Mes amis viennent me voir, ce qui est déjà beaucoup. Il m'est impossible

Half-Way House, Rottingdean

d'écrire et difficile de lire. J'adore recevoir des lettres, plus que tout, des lettres de vous.

Cher Monsieur l'Abbé, priez pour moi.

Votre humblement dévoué,

Maurice Baring.

(signed) M. B.

Half-Way House, Steyning Road, Rottingdean

20th February, 1937

To Sir Ronald Storrs

My dear Ronald,

All success to your civic career.

Thank you for the Catullus. I suppose this is where the phrase, "A name writ in water" first occurs?

I return the two letters. I thought myself when I read the first chapters you showed me (not the ones you showed me last) that the book needed pruning, was swamped at times in detail; and one was sometimes uneasily conscious of a *cinema* effect of being jerked suddenly from close-ups to whatever non-close-ups are called. All books, to my mind, now suffer from being written too quickly. Kipling, in his autobiography just published, has some wise remarks on pruning.

I now appeal to your scholarship; Iliad, Book 22, lines 466-472. If one translates the first lines with the big Liddell and Scott, the words about the various details of the head-dress are all the same. Thus, when you get "From her head she threw off the shining head-band, the net and the head-band and the woven wreath and the veil". Lang, etc., translate it like this: "From off her head she shook the bright attiring thereof,

frontlet and net and woven band, and the veil."
A. T. Murray translates it like this: "From off her head
she cast the bright attiring thereof, the frontlet and
coif and kerchief and woven band, and the veil etc. . . ."
Church, in his *Stories from Homer*, beautifully abridges it
and writes: "And from her fair head dropped the net and
the wreath and the diadem." He leaves out the veil,
which is a pity I think.

But what I want to get is, does Ampuka mean frontlet?
And if so does "frontlet" mean the kind of Greek diadem
Rachel is seen with in her photograph when playing
Phædra? I dislike the word "frontlet" immensely;
can one translate it "diadem"? What I want is before
quoting Church's beautiful paraphrase, a word for word
literal translation, but it is no use saying *band* six times
running, and still worse to use technical terms which
are wrong.

Ethel came here the other day and was splendid.
Wishing you all success.

Yours, M. B.

Half-Way House, Steyning Road, Rottingdean
5th June, 1937

To Sir Ronald Storrs

My dear Ronald,
Thank you for your interim enquiry. I am "still in
the body"—all too much so.

My doctors have become like Chinese Puzzle boxes,
but it is *their* doing not mine. Plesch, whose name you
spell wrong, when he had finished with me put me on

to a man called Martin, who, in his turn called in the aid of Gonin. Between the three they cured me of Neuritis, and agreed that they had done all that orthodox medicine could do towards alleviating *Paralysis Agitans,* and that there was nothing more to do but chance the unorthodox.

Bernard Shaw told Ethel about Alexander, and I am going to him. He has done me good in some ways. As it is, I have better days but worse nights, and I am not too old to learn the new tricks which he teaches. I think his theories are sound, and I agree with Bernard Shaw in thinking him a genius. He sadly lacks the gift of expression, for although extremely fluent I find him difficult to understand.

I listened in to Ethel's Mass till the atmospherics interfered. I thought it most noble.

I have got the book about Lawrence, and I have read the greater part of it. That part which was written by people who know how to write was, strange to say, the more readable, and among those the one who wrote best was your esteemed self.

In the Index talking of the "Gepäck" he says the bulk of it consists of mutilated copies of the *Oxford Books of Verse.* Is this true? I rather think *not,* for the simple reason that the *Oxford Books of Verse* are printed on paper which is too thin for the purpose of Gepäck making, but as I have made so many I forget. For the making of the earlier Gepäcks hundreds of books were slaughtered. I got more cunning as the time went on and more economical.

Are you going to the Glyndebourne Opera?

Yours, *M. B.*

Sent to M. l'Abbé Mugnier and found in his papers.

18, *Cheyne Row, Chelsea, S.W.*3

Anecdote raconté par le peintre Anglais Burne-Jones

"L'autre jour un prêtre à Avignon confessait ses pénitents. Il aperçut parmi les fidèles un jeune homme splendide, fort et sauvage, le cou large, les cheveux d'or, et très grand. Le jeune homme attendit son tour et s'agenouilla le dernier au confessional. Il confessa tant de crimes que le prêtre lui dit: "Mais vous avez dû vivre pendant des siècles pour avoir fait tant de mal."

"J'ai vêcu des milliers d'années", répondit le jeune homme: "je suis tombé du ciel à la naissance du monde, et je voudrais y retourner."

Le prêtre répondit que cela pouvait se faire. Il dit:

"Répétez après moi: 'Dieu seul est grand et parfait.'"

Et le jeune homme s'en alla encore désolé, encore damné.

Half-Way House, Steyning Road, Rottingdean
le 24 septembre 1938

To Monsieur l'Abbé Mugnier de Nôtre Dame, Paris
Cher Monsieur l'Abbé,

J'étais enchanté de recevoir deux cartes postales portant votre signature.

Le monde est bien méchant en ce moment. Je viens de relire "Les Mémoires d'Outre-Tombe". La phrase suivante me console:

"Toujours dans l'histoire marchent ensemble deux choses; qu'un homme s'ouvre une voie d'injustice, il s'ouvre en même temps une voie de perdition dans laquelle, à une distance marquée, la première route vient tomber dans la seconde."

Agréez, je vous prie, Monsieur l'Abbé, l'expression de mon affection respectueusement dévouée.

Maurice Baring.

Half-Way House, Steyning Road, Rottingdean
30th November, 1939

To R. Hart Davies, Esq.

Dear Rupert,

It is a treat to get a letter from you. The couplet in question is correctly quoted. It occurs in "C" (as you know), page 423, when "C" and his friends are capping quotations. The text runs as follows:—

"Hallam interrupted and said:

'Do you know this?—

It is not many miles to Mantua,

No further than the end of this mad world.'

Nobody knew and Hallam said he had forgotten."

It is not surprising that nobody knew because I invented the lines myself. I always thought of them as a part of a duologue between Romeo and Juliet, Juliet saying the first line and Romeo the second. But they were not written by Shakespeare.

Books. I am always glad of books. The trouble with me is size and shape. I cannot manage tall or fat books. I can't hold any book in my hands, and I can only manage books that open flat on my reading desk. What is best for me are unbound books, page proofs.

Yours,

M. B.

Eilean Aigas, Beauly, Scotland
To Sir Ronald Storrs   1st January, 1941

Dear Ronald,

Thank you for your Christmas wishes, and I wish you a happy New Year. Nurse is away; I took the Sortes Virgilianae at the beginning of the war. Once for the war and once for Mussolini and Hitler. I haven't got the references here, but the first was to the effect that fire would be rained down from Heaven, the second and third, Mussolini and Hitler, came out on *the same page and the same line,* and it was to the effect that they would be led to the Tarpeian rock.

Best, love,

M. B.

Beaufort Castle, Beauly, Scotland
To Sir Claud Russell   2nd April, 1945

Dear Claud,

Thank you very much for your letter. I learned from the Press that Treves is the oldest city in Europe. Is this true? There is another Church that claims to possess fragments of the Coat without Seam, namely, that of Argenteuil. I think it was separated into pieces, and hidden during the French Revolution. This church still claims to have portions of it. I send you a

74

post-card with a picture of what they have got. I
looked it all up when I was writing my book *Coat
Without Seam,* and, as far as I remember, there was
never any pronouncement on the authenticity of these
relics; they were both very old, and both places claimed
a tradition. In any case, the authenticity of either would
not be a matter of Faith, but a pious opinion.

I didn't have Ackroyd's book about the Cuckoo
Mystery long enough to understand his thesis. Are you
a "beaker" or a "layer"? I am sorry Conrad hasn't been
well.

Best love,

Yours,

M. B.

PS. I have just looked up what I wrote in my book
Coat Without Seam (I have only a copy in Spanish). In
the book, the village Curé of an imaginary place
(founded on Argenteuil) says that the Relic is a Holy
Vestment that was believed for many years to be the
Coat Without Seam, for which the soldiers drew lots;
and many pilgrims came to see it, although its
authenticity was doubtful, and the inhabitants of
Treves claimed to possess the Holy Coat in their
Cathedral, and to have received it from the Empress
Helena in the fourth century, and it is probable that
our relic which we received from Charlemagne, is not
the Coat.

Others have called our Relic the *Capa Pueri Jesu,*
that is to say, the Coat of the Child Jesus. During the
Revolution, when it was in another church, the Curé
cut it into four pieces, and hid it, for fear of its being

taken. In 1795 some of the pieces were recovered. One of the characters then asks the Curé whether the stories of relics are true; and he answers what I have already said about pious opinion, and adds a little more about the nature of tradition, and about its not being necessary to believe in the authenticity of the relic. He adds that the Treves tradition may be the true one, and is undoubtedly older than the French tradition.

M. B.

A letter from Miss Sylvia Tatham

<table>
<tr><td>To Laura, Lady Lovat</td><td>Northcourt House, Abingdon, Berks
11th July, 1946</td></tr>
</table>

Dear Madam,

Mr. Maurice Baring was a pupil of my father's here, in this house, in, I think, 1892 or 1893. He and my father used to write Triolets to each other; some of these were printed in small books, *Northcourt Nonsense* and *Triolets;* (a copy of the former, Mr. Baring told us, was sold at Sotheby's for £36 in 1929). They continued corresponding in Triolets from time to time until only a few years before my father's death in 1937.

The first Triolet letter from M.B. to my father, M. T. Tatham, printed in *Northcourt Nonsense* is as follows:—

May I wear a silk tie
Tonight at the table?
I've been stung by a fly,
May I wear a silk tie?

I will bind it as high
And as low as I'm able
May I wear a silk tie
Tonight at the table?

'Twas the sting of a fly
And I vow it's no fable;
I feel ready to cry;
'Twas the sting of a fly,
And I feel as if I
Had been Cained by an Abel;
'Twas the sting of a fly,
And I vow it's no fable.

And my father's answer was:—

The tie that you wear
May be wholly of silk
Or of stuff or mohair,
The tie that you wear;
If the pain you can't bear,
Better bathe it with milk,
The tie that you wear
May be wholly of silk.

The following is a "proposed letter to the Dean of
Christ Church" by M. B.:—

My pupil is ill,
Will you cause him to pass?
He caught a bad chill;
My pupil is ill ;

He afterwards will
Take a classic first class
My pupil is ill,
Will you cause him to pass?

"Supposed postcard written by the Dean of Christ Church in answer to the Triolet above." (Mr. Baring says, "The pupil was no other than Augustus Ralli, the eminent fencer, who unfortunately caught rheumatic fever, with quadratic complications, and was obliged to make a short trip to the Alcaic Islands for change of air.")

Our Term is commencing,
No time to be lost;
Is he skilful at fencing?
Our Term is commencing;
My style I'm condensing
Because of the cost;
Our Term is commencing
No time to be lost.

After Mr. Baring left us and went to Cambridge, the Triolets continued in telegrams.

Yours faithfully,

(*Miss*) *Sylvia Tatham.*

To M. T. Tatham, Esq.   *No date*

Dear Mr. Tatham,

It was very amusing to get such a letter this morning. (At 2). It *was* very amusing. And after perusing it I felt much better. It was *very* amusing to get such a letter. Your pain *must* have been great in that corridor coach. When it grew cold and late, your pain must have been great. And not even a date! No preserves there to *poach*—your pain must have been great in that corridor coach. Weren't you ready to cry? There was nothing to broach in that corridor coach. As you neared the approach of Penzance (close to Skye?). In that corridor coach weren't you ready to cry, "We're arriving at last! Let us wipe the wet eye! Weren't you ready to cry: At the Island of Skye and the town of Belfast, weren't you read to cry "We're arriving at last?"

I've been trying all day to resolve an equation. They all think it's child's play; I've been trying all day. And I've shown (so they say) signs of great irritation; I've been *trying* all day to resolve an equation—to resolve an equation is very poor sport. It needs much contemplation to resolve an equation; there's a new complication in every new sort; to resolve an equation is very poor sport.

I don't think that I left any books at your mansion? Nor what Germans call "Heft"? I don't think that I left my new treatise on Theft or my "Seely's" Expansion. I don't *think* that I left my books at your mansion. I don't want them again. None, except Catriona. That is perfectly plain. *I* don't want them again. Let them rest and remain with a suitable owner. I don't want them again—none except Catriona.

Are you Provost of King's or the Master of Trinity? They are quite different things. Are you Provost of King's? They are clothed with white wings and they talk of divinity. Are you Provost of King's or the Master of Trinity?

Please to greet Messrs. Crum, Jenkins, Sidgwick and Ralli with the roll of the drum; please to greet Messrs. Crum. Now I *must* do my sum. Don't forget with "Ho,

79

Tally" to greet Messrs. Crum, Jenkins, Sidgwick and Ralli.
So I beg to remain your devoted "M. B." They say
he's insane. *So I beg to remain.* I shall soon come by
train just for afternoon tea; so I beg to remain.

Yours devoted,

M. B.

3 *Gray's Inn Square, W.C.*1

To M. T. Tatham, Esq.   1*st June,* 1899

Oh, do not call me 'Mister'
If you write again,
It annoys me like a blister
Oh do not call me 'Mister'.
I am not Owen Wister
Nor Mr. Loraine
Oh do not call me 'Mister'
If you write again
You'll observe I obey
Your infectious refrain
'Dear Tatham' I say
You'll observe I obey
And I'll write if I may
Yet again and again.
You'll observe I obey
Your infectious refrain.

Dear Tatham,
A thousand thanks. The trouble is I have not the
Latin text any more, and don't know where to find it.
I was staying in a house where it was. The text there
seemed to me if I remember right to leave out some
word, and one of these words you have put in, namely,

80

"senseless". How do you translate "acer" in the last
sentence if it is there? Does it mean spirited, full of
spirit? In the sentence "Since he received from his
victorious enemy a treatment no more severely cruel
than he would have inflicted on that enemy if he had
been in his place", the *he* and *his* cannot help being
ambiguous. Mark Twain used to say when this happened,
damn the English language, but couldn't one get round
this by saying something like "had the circumstances
been reversed".

Please express my regard
I will send her a card
From his lordship of Latham,
Please express my regard
To my dear Mrs. Tatham.

Telegrams to Mrs. Tatham.　　　　*27th September*, 1893

1.　　　Are you eating a goose?
　　　It's the feast of St. Michael,
　　　With stuffing and juice
　　　If not you are loose
　　　As regards the year's cycle.
　　　Are you eating a goose
　　　On the feast of St. Michael?

2.　　　My lines do not scan
　　　I most heartily grieve
　　　Quite smooth once they ran
　　　My lines do not scan
　　　For the telegraph man
　　　Refused to abrieve
　　　My lines do not scan.

81

III

Verse

ON FATHER VINCENT MCNABB'S DEATH

Published in the memorial edition of "Blackfriars", 1941

("I once had a letter from a New Zealander who wrote a beautiful book—not a Catholic. He attended one of Father Vincent's conferences, and wrote the enclosed, on which I base what I send you. . . . 'March 1931. I have twice heard Father Vincent preach. It was each time the most exquisite, intimate, unique experience. When he began in his halting and wandering way I was disappointed; but in five minutes I had learnt to attune my ear, and my attention was closely held. I was entranced, and hardly felt human when I came away —I felt so light—that is memorable; the lightness—the taking flight that had happened—something divine. . . . I noticed that he often did not remember the exact words of his text, or of many parts of the Bible— when he wanted to repeat them—but must find and read them anew. He was so filled with remembering that the actual words meant nothing to him—but their meaning only. Now I have had at last heard what I have always longed to hear—a man inspired. D'A.C.' ")

A poet heard you preach and told me this:
While listening to your argument unwind
He seemed to leave the heavy world behind;
And liberated in a bright abyss
All burdens and all load and weight to shed;
Uplifted like a leaf before the wind,
Untrammelled in a region unconfined,
He moved as lightly as the happy dead.
And as you read the message of our Lord
You stumbled over the familiar word,
As if the news now sudden to you came;
As if you stood upon the holy ground
Within the house filled with the mighty sound
And lit with Pentecostal tongues of flame.

TO WINSTON

You promised only blood and sweat and tears
And lifted up our hearts, and drowned our fears.

FRAGMENTS

Nothing shall come of nothing; speak again!
Still, out of nothing God made time and place,
The sun, the stars, the Summer and your face.

Dark trees, the silver river, twilight skies
A tawny moon and your celestial eyes.

I have known beauty, and I once was young
But you are more than all the poets sung.

Various in beauty, versatile as flame,
And never save in constancy the same.

Thank you for your words and days;
Silver speech and golden phrase.

TO ETHEL SMYTH

Your singing brings the rustle of the trees,
The tall trees sighing on the mountain-side;
It brings a whisper from the foamless tide
That broadening fills the ample estuaries.

Your singing brings the freshness of the breeze
That comes at twilight to the breathless plain;
The cry of moaning ghosts that call in vain
From wandering prisons in the winds and seas.

Your singing brings to me the final peace,
Dissolves the torment of perplexity
And guides my spirit to a tranquil home;
As when the moon compels the storm to cease
And calms the wind; and all the skeins of foam
Unravel softly on the vanquished sea.

SONG

The day breaks and the darkness taketh flight,
The north wind blows upon the rippling sea;
My locks are dripping with the dews of night.
My Dawn, my Daylight, open thou to me.

The spices of thy garden fill the air,
The blossom glistens on thine apple-tree;
Sweeter than spice art thou, than flowers more fair.
My Dew, my Blossom, open thou to me.

Come, let us seek the mountains of the myrrh,
The hills of frankincense, the fragrant sea;
The north wind blows, the leaves, the water stir.
My Dove, my Springtide, open thou to me.

THE WOUNDED

To H. C.

They turn us from the long-desired door;
Here there is shelter for the sorely spent,
But not for us; since many a dying score
Of maimed and mangled men, whose limbs are rent

With bayonet and with bullet, crowd the floor.
We who have fought since dawn, nor tasted bread,
Although our wounds are slight, our wounds are sore,
We must march on, nor shall we find a bed.

O men, O brothers, is our rest not earned?
Shall we not seek the mountains huge and wide
Whose doors are always open? There the guest

Sweet welcome finds; for thou hast never turned
A stranger from thy gates, nor hast denied,
O hospitable Death, a place to rest.

Fun-chu-ling,

THE DEAD SAMURAI TO DEATH

To E. C.

I had not called nor prayed for thee to come;
No favour of the Fates I bent to ask,
I thought but of the momentary task:
In the supreme bright hour my soul was dumb.

Yet above all the rest 'twas here and now
I longed to meet with thee, O beckoning friend;
Before the lighting of thine eyes to bow
And follow thee to where the triumphs end.

Therefore let those who gaze upon me here
Discern no sadness in my staring eyes
And no regret; they will not look for fear.

I dared not hope to meet thee in this place;
The let my smile speak rapture and surprise
And with ineffable wonder stamp my face.

Poutiloff's Hill,

THE DYING RESERVIST

To B. C.

I shall not see the faces of my friends,
Nor hear the songs the rested reapers sing
After the labours of the harvesting,
In those dark nights before the Summer ends;

Nor see the floods of Spring, the melting snow,
Nor in the Autumn twilight hear the stir
Of reedy marshes, when the wild ducks whir
And circle black against the afterglow.

My Mother died; she shall not have to weep;
My wife will find another home; my child,
Too young, will never grieve or know; but I

Have found my brother, and contentedly
I'll lay my head upon his knees and sleep.
O brother Death—I knew you when you smiled.

ON THE DEATH OF WILLY THE MOON, WHO FOR THIRTY YEARS CLEANED AND LIT THE LAMPS AT BEAUFORT CASTLE

If you're wanting a job to be done well and soon
The man who can do it is Willy the Moon.
He works all the day, and he gives of his best,
But now he is surely in need of a rest.
It's no use a-calling; he's far, far away,
He's trimming the lamps on the wide Milky Way.
All the pipers of Heaven will strike up a tune
Of welcome to Willy, dear Willy the Moon.

THE LAST CRUISE OF H.M.S "TIGER",
26th MARCH, 1931

"Mate, when does *Tiger* weigh?"
Said the V.A.
And nevermore
By flag or semaphore
That signal can be made, by flag or flame:
For Battle Cruiser *Tiger*, thirteenth warship of that
    name,
For Battle Cruiser *Tiger* is sailing home today
To be scrapped and thrown away.

Goodbye, Gibraltar. There's the usual swell,
And in the air that spicy Spanish smell.
Gibraltar knows the name of *Tiger* well,
For *Tiger* helped to take and defend
The Rock against the changing foe,
Before she went to her long 'make and mend'
Somewhere beneath the Gulf of Mexico.

Sunrise on the Atlantic: all is peace:
And through soft shreds of ravelled fleece
The rosy sun like some exotic flower
Unfolds its glory to the breathless hour.
Later the sea has a smile as smooth as glass;
But sailors know that silken smile too well—
The passing favour of a fickle lass,
The harbinger of fog and moaning bell.
But now the breeze has blown the mist away
Across the Bay.

"Attack by Aircraft" is the Exercise,
As from above the skies
Comes a faint ping,
Slight as the whirring of a beetles wing:
Now come the little specks upon the blue,
Now larger spots; now seaplanes not a few:
And now a deafening roar,
And down upon the ships they swoop and soar.

It's Saturday night at sea, and so tonight,
Although they've darkened ship there will be light
(*Tiger, Tiger,* burning bright',
When they darken ship at night)
Within the Wardroom Mess
(It's 'Mess Undress')
On silver trophies and on rattling knives:
The while they drink to Sweethearts and to Wives.

As bright as a new pin or silver pound
Tiger is cheering ship in Plymouth Sound.
Exultant in her finery,
Like a young Spartan going out to die.
"For scrap-heap or no scrap-heap, as long as she's
        afloat,"
The Captain said, "upon my ship they shan't
        detect a mote",
To which the ship made suitable reply;
"We don't think", or in other words, "Aye, Aye."

Tiger, to greet you there were mighty ghosts,
And silent signals from immortal hosts,
Tiger who sailed with Drake to tropic seas,

And chased the Spaniard to the Hebrides,
Tiger who bade the Spanish *Tigre* surrender
(*Tiger* who saw no service was a Tender)
Tiger the sloop, the first to steam (God bless her)
Sunk by the Russian forts outside Odessa,
Tiger who in an Exercise at night
Sank in collision off the Isle of Wight,
And those who in this *Tiger* fought and died
At Jutland, came to see you over the side.

Now *Tiger* has crept back into her lair,
She will not go a-fighting any more;
And there are few who know and less that care.
But there are some whose hearts are very sore.

They'll skin her of her coat and break her neck,
And spoil her brasswork and her spotless deck,
Her purring padding engines (Tigers proper!)
And every shining piece of steel and copper
For all that pomp and power of black and gold,
Drenched in story,
Scarred with glory,
Must now be broken up and sold,
And broken up and sold or thrown away,
And *Tiger* shall not live to fight another day.
For *Tiger*, once the flagship of Lord Beatty,
Must now be scrapped forthwith, so says the Treaty.
And once upon the scrap heap, not all the King's
        men
Will ever put *Tiger* together again;
Not all the King's horses; not all the King's men.

"QUAND VOUS SEREZ BIEN VIEILLE"

When you are old, no man will start to hear
That you were once more lovely than the day;
Old age may change but cannot take away
From you; and you will meet him without fear.

Yet when you think of him who loved fair things
And singing of all beauty sang but you,
Nor dreamed you guessed the secret of his strings,
Then say: "Although he knew it not, I knew."

I shall be dead and mid the shadowy throng
In the long twilight I shall not forget;
You still shall tread the earth with royal grace;

And if you smile remembering my song,
A moonbeam to the kingdoms of regret
Will come and flood with light the sunless place.

DEDICATION

(*Translated from the German of Goethe*)

Once more, you hovering phantoms, gather round,
That long ago bedimmed my youthful eyes!
And shall I try this time to keep you bound?
Am I bewitched by that mad Paradise?
You crowd upon me! Have your way! Be crowned
And rule, as you from mist about me rise;
My heart, grown young again, is beating fast,
Touched by the spell you breathe as you go past.

You bring me visions of unclouded time,
And many a dear familiar ghost I see;
Like some old legend's distant, dying chime;
First love and friendship come in company;
Pain smarts afresh, once more the plangent rhyme
Unwinds the devious maze life chose for me,
And names the Good whom turning Chance bereft
Of happiness, and me to mourn them left.

They cannot hear the aftermath of song,
The souls for whom I first began to sing;
Dispersed and vanished is the living throng,
And silent echo's first responsive ring.
My gifts to alien multitudes belong,
Whose very cheers but leave me shuddering;
And all to whom my song once gave delight,
If still alive, are scattered out of sight.

And long unfelt desire now draws me near
To that still, solemn realm of ghostly shade;

My song in dim diminished tones I hear
Lisp like a harp that by the wind is played;
I tremble, and tear follows hot on tear,
And the stern heart grows soft and half afraid;
The present as a distant dream I see,
And the dead past is now alive to me.

Persian pomp offends me, boy,
Linden-ribboned wreaths annoy,
Search me not the garden close
For a late October rose.
Crowns of myrtle leaf will do,
One for me and one for you,
When you pour me out the wine,
When I drink beneath the vine.

TROPARION

(Translated from the Russian of Count Alexis Tolstoy)

What joy does earthly life possess
That hath no part in earthly sorrow?
What joy that proves not false tomorrow?
Where among men is happiness?
Of all that we through toil obtain
Nothing is lasting, all is vain—
What glories on the earth are sure
And steadfast and unchanged endure?
All is but shadow, dream, and sand,
And like a whirlwind blows away,
And face to face with Death we stand
Unarmed in helpless disarray.
The right hand of the mighty one
Is nothing, naught the king's command—
Lord, now thy servant's life is done,
Receive him in Thy blessèd land.

Death like a warrior hot with pride
Waylaid and like a robber felled me,
The grave its jaws hath opened wide,
From all that liveth hath withheld me.
Be saved my children and my kin,
From the grave hear my warning knell,
Brothers and friends be saved from sin
So you escape the flames of hell.
Life is but vanity throughout,
And at the scent of death's decay
Like unto flowers we fade away—
Why do we vainly toss about?

The grave is what was once a throne,
Our palaces a heap of sand—
Lord, now Thy servant's life is done,
Receive him in Thy blessèd land.

Who midst the bones in rotting heap
Is warrior, judge, or king or slave?
Who shall be numbered with the sheep,
Who the rejected evil knave?
Where is the silver and the gold,
O Brothers, where the hosts of slaves?
And who among the nameless graves
The rich and poor beneath the mould?
All is but smoke and dust and ash,
A dream, a shade, a phantom flash—
Lord, but in Thy bright Paradise
Our refuge and salvation lies.
All that was flesh beneath the sun
Shall fade, our pomps shall rot in sand—
Lord, now Thy servant's life is done,
Receive him in Thy blessèd land.

And Thou who for the world does weep,
Thou, Advocate of the oppressed,
We cry to Thee, The Holiest,
For Him our brother here asleep.
Pray to Thy God-begotten Son,
Pray, O, most pure of womankind
That now our Brother's life is done
He leaves his sorrows here behind.
All is but smoke, and dust, and wraith,
O friends, in phantoms put no faith!

When we upon some sudden day
Shall scent the breath of death's decay,
We shall be stricken every one,
Like corn beneath the reaper's hand—
Lord, now Thy servant's life is done,
Receive him in Thy blessèd land.

I travel on a road unknown,
Half hopeful, half in fear I go.
My sight is dim, my heart a stone,
My lips are sealed, my hearing slow,
And motionless, bereft of speech,
I cannot hear the brethren wail,
And out of sight and out of reach
The censer's blue and fragrant veil;
But till in endless sleep I fall,
My love shall never pass away.
And by that love I, brethren, pray
That each thus unto God shall call:
Lord, on that day when moon and sun
Shall vanish at the trump's command—
Now that Thy servant's life is done,
Receive him in Thy blessèd land.

Senior Novitiate Library

THE PROPHET

(Translated from the Russian of A. S. Pushkin)

With fainting soul athirst for Grace,
I wandered in a desert place,
And at the crossing of the ways
I saw the sixfold Seraph blaze;
He touched mine eyes with fingers light
As sleep that cometh in the night:
And like a frighted eagle's eyes
They opened wide with prophecies.
He touched mine ears, and they were drowned
With tumult and a roaring sound:
I heard convulsion in the sky,
And flights of angel hosts on high,
And beasts that move beneath the sea,
And the sap creeping in the tree.
And bending to my mouth he wrung
From out of it my sinful tongue,
And all its lies and idle rust,
And 'twixt my lips a-perishing
A subtle serpent's forkèd sting
With right hand wet with blood he thrust.
And with his sword my breast he cleft,
My quaking heart thereout he reft,
An in the yawning of my breast
A coal of living fire he pressed.
Then in the desert I lay dead,
And God called unto me and said:
"Arise, and let My Voice be heard;
Charged with My Will go forth and span
The land and sea, and let My Word
Lay waste with fire the heart of man."

(Translated from the Russian of A. S. Pushkin)

I loved you: and perhaps my love today
Has not yet died away.
Howbeit, that shall no more trouble you;
I would not have you rue,
I loved you utterly remote and dumb,
Jealous; o'ercome;
I loved you with so true a tenderness—
God grant another may not love you less!

TESTAMENT

(Translated from the Russian of M. Y. Lermontov)

I want to be alone with you,
A moment quite alone.
The minutes left to me are few,
They say I'll soon be gone.
And you are going home on leave,
Then say . . . but why? I do believe
There's not a soul who'll greatly care
To hear about me over there.

And yet if someone questions you,
Whoever it may be,—
Tell them a bullet hit me through
The chest,—and did for me.
And say I died, and for the Tsar,
And say what fools the doctors are:—
And that I shook you by the hand,
And spoke about my native land.

My father and my mother, both,
By now are surely dead—
To tell the truth, I would be loth
To send them tears to shed.
If one of them is living, say
I'm bad at writing home, and they
Have told the regiment to pack,—
And that I shan't be coming back.

We had a neighbour, as you know,
And you remember I

And she. . . . How very long ago
It is we said goodbye!
She won't ask after me, nor care,
But tell her ev'rything, don't spare
Her empty heart; and let her cry,—
To her it doesn't signify.

VALE

I am for ever haunted by one dread
That I may suddenly be swept away,
Nor have the leave to see you and to say
Goodbye; then this is what I would have said:

I have loved Summer and the longest day:
The leaves of June, the slumbrous film of heat,
The bees, the swallow, and the waving wheat,
The whistling of the mowers in the hay.

I have loved words which lift the soul with wings,
Words that are windows to eternal things;
I have loved souls that to themselves are true,

Who cannot stoop and know not how to fear,
Yet hold the talisman of pity's tear;
I have loved these because I have loved you.

Half-Way House, Rottingdean

IV

On the Effect of the Classics on Maurice Baring's Mind

by RONALD A. KNOX

TO HEAR Maurice Baring described as a classical scholar is to be conscious of words used, for better or worse, in a wrong sense. He had, to be sure, something of the scholar's temperament. In particular he could not bear to leave a problem unsolved if it bore on language or on the interpretation of a man's thought, however insignificant the point involved. He would write to you suddenly demanding an elucidation, and when you had done your best, would follow it up with a fusillade of supplementary questions, filling your post-bag for a week or ten days. There was some passage, for example, in Sir Edward Marsh's admirable translation of Horace which suggested a query to him; and this particular correspondence developed, before long, into a passionate enquiry as to the precise meaning of the word "bast", and the precise uses to which the article so described could be put. On another occasion I find I was brought in to do him a rendering, in Latin and Greek verse, of Rossetti's line, "You could not tell the starlings from the leaves"; I have no idea why he wanted it.

All this may sound mere eccentricity, but it did betoken a real meticulousness about getting things right, as well as a certain restlessness in his psychology. I remember his spending a whole morning poking about among the strange assortment of books in the old library at Beaufort (now ashes); his object was to discover whether the railway got as far as Rome, or still stopped short at Turin, at the time when Blanche first visited Rome in *Cat's Cradle*. Not one reader in a thousand would have caught him out if he had got it wrong, but (if only because a story, for him, always took on the colours of real life) he could not bear to make Blanche achieve the impossible. He *wrote* easily (as all his readers rightly infer), but the detailed building-up of a story, the dresses the women ought to wear, and the menu which ought to grace a particular luncheon-party, cost him hours of conscientious application. In all this, there was a kind of intellectual fastidiousness which might have made him free of any Common-room.

Yet he would not have claimed to be a classical scholar; nor did anybody ever claim more loudly that he had neglected the opportunities for a classical training which school and university (we are speaking of the last century) provided. On the contrary, he imposed it on himself as a kind of morbid duty to meet all the efforts of the educationalist with steady sales-resistance; readers of Chesterton's autobiography will remember that he, too, deliberately shunned every temptation to win school prizes. The beginning of *Friday's Business* is, I imagine, an exact reflection not only of what those school days were like, but of what Maurice's attitude was like; dons and schoolmasters were there, not so that you could learn from them, but so that you could rag them. He professed to have carried away from Eton only one piece of information about the classical world, namely, the meaning of the Latin word *manubiae*. He was very proud of knowing that it meant, not "booty" but "money derived from the sale of booty".

There are, however, certain rare intellects which aspire to a sublime ignorance in vain. They cannot choose but learn. Maurice's nature was one which constantly absorbed, as it constantly exuded, something which (for want of a less abused word) you can only label "culture". The least absorbed, he was the most retentive of readers. And I picture him, at school, as one of the rare oppidans one used to see hanging about School Library, then a rather dreary suite of rooms in the New Schools. There were only two or three of them, always the same ones, and they seemed to pull books out of shelves all over the place with a remarkably omnivorous taste. I can see Maurice doing this—quite lost to the sense of time—on rainy after-fours; but whether he really did so I have no idea. If not, the classics he read in form must have got under his skin, I suppose, without his noticing it. For, whether it was the mind of a scholar or no, his mind was soaked in the classics.

No doubt he read the classical authors—the poets anyhow—as a grown man. There is his own account, for example, of how he met a goat-herd on a lonely Greek island, and tried him with a volume of Sappho which happened to be in his pocket. The goat-herd (so Maurice declared) read one or two of the poems through, and handed the book back with the comment, "Ah, *patois*." Anyhow, the idea of having Sappho in your pocket did not strike Maurice as unusual. Yet, when I knew him, in the last thirty years of his life, I do not remember seeing him read a classical author; nor were they noticeably frequent on his shelves at Rottingdean. And in any case it is almost impossible to be soaked in the classics unless you are caught young. Meredith's well chosen tags and happy allusions do not really convince; you are conscious of the classical dictionary at his elbow; but Maurice took it all in his stride, as he did everything from liturgy to prize-fighting. And it is very hard to take the classics in your stride unless they are effectively interwoven with your own memories of boyhood.

It would be easy, when so much is said, to conjure up the picture of an old-fashioned country gentleman who spices his conversation with an occasional *Eheu fugaces* or *Facilis descensus Averno* to show that he can do it. From Maurice's conversation, always utterly unaffected, it would be more likely to leak out that he knew Russian, than that he knew Latin. He avows himself that Catullus lived for him more than Horace; and this he can hardly have owed to Eton in days when Dr. Warre drummed Horace into us, and Macnaghten was not yet (I imagine) in a position to make Eton boys fall in love with the music of Sirmio. I have often wondered, but never asked, whether "C" was consciously the story of Catullus re-written, as Darby and Joan was Mary Queen of Scots re-written (one of its reviewers said the thing could not have happened in real life). A psychologist would pounce on the similarity between the names Catullus and Caryll, the names Lesbia and Leila, as proof of unconscious association. But, then, it would have been very like Maurice to do it on purpose by way of scoring off the psychologist.

Be that as it may, those early books of his which were afterwards bound together under the title *Unreliable History* are heavily overweighted on the classical side. More than half of the Diminutive Dramas, more than a third of the Lost Letters, and a quarter of the Lost Diaries, have a classical setting. Nor do I think he was ever better inspired than when he thus played on the eternal themes in Greek or Latin dress. "Ariadne in Naxos", for instance, and "From the Mycenæ papers", give you his minute observation of the opposite sex almost better than his novels do. The utter simplicity of the décor suited his genius. And I never remember discovering, or having pointed out to me, a single lapse of scholarship in the whole of the three volumes.

But perhaps the most striking proof of his love for antiquity came at the very end of his literary career. When it became evident that his lingering illness would make it impossible for him to go on with the exhausting business of authorship, I made a suggestion which proved uncannily fruitful—that he should select some material from his commonplace books and work it up, with a little editing, into an anthology. *Have You Anything to Declare?* is to some people the most cherished of his books. And one extraordinary thing about it is that roughly a third of the material in it dates back before Dante. Of course, he may have chosen too many of those earlier extracts, not guessing how long the book would be. Yet it is surely remarkable that a man so widely read in English literature, and in the literature of five other great modern languages, should have made such a generous allowance for the Latin and Greek to which his Eton form-masters would have pronounced him impervious. The truth is, I think, that he took an exceptional delight in *translation*; in the delicate shades of difference which manifest themselves when the same idea is perfectly expressed first in one language and then in another. And from this point of view Latin and Greek stand apart by themselves, because their whole idiom is so unlike ours. If it be scholarship to take an almost gluttonous delight in the deft manipulation by which an idea, or set of ideas, is taken out of one language and put into another, to that extent he was a scholar.

Yet more I think he was, in the literary sense of the word, a humanist. He went largely, no doubt, to the Romantics for his inspiration. But there was a restraint about everything he wrote which is utterly classical. I do not say he owed it to the reading of the classics; it may have been due to something in his own nature; but it made the classics congenial to him. I doubt if you would have said, even when he had finished cramming at Scoones', that he had *learned* Latin and Greek. But, with a sure instinct, he breathed the airs of them.

V

Letter to Laura Lady Lovat from Princess Marthe Bibesco

AS a postscript to this book I would like to add Princess Marthe Bibesco's answer to my request that she should write a preface to the French translation of "Passing By", Maurice's first novel, and the one on which his dying mind had concentrated in so remarkable a manner. Its beauty needs no comment.

Ma chère Laure,

J'espérais vous voir écrire cette préface. Nulle mieux que vous ne pouvait attirer sur le roman de Maurice Baring la sympathie des lecteurs français; vous l'aviez inspiré; il vous est dédié; vous étiez faite pour présenter l'auteur à ceux qui ne l'ont pas connu et qui voudraient entreprendre avec lui ce voyage au pays de l'autre, qu'est un bon livre. Entre vous qui saviez tout de lui, et moi qui n'en sais presque rien, le choix était facile. Mais votre lettre est venue; vous m'avez substituée à vous, bien malgré moi, avec cette grâce d'attitude à laquelle personne de vos amis n'a jamais résisté. On a dit très justement de Maurice Baring que la vie n'était jamais devenue pour lui une habitude, qu'elle était toujours restée un miracle, et ce fut vrai, jusqu'à la fin. Cet écrivain de race, ce fantaisiste facétieux, cet attaché d'ambassade, détaché à la Royal Air Force en 1914, cet esprit inspiré, cet ingénieux conteur qui fut à la fois un poète et un personnage poétique, après avoir consacré sa vie aux Lettres et à l'amitié, vous l'apporta comme un ex-voto, lorsqu'il vint mourir chez vous, en catholique pour qui l'acte de remettre son âme à Dieu est un acte d'amour, accompli en pleine conscience et dans la joie.

Je suis Prêt, la devise française qui se voit partout et jusque sur le Saint Ciboire de votre chapelle au château de Beaufort, en Ecosse, a servi de mot de passe à votre hôte lorsqu'il a quitté ce monde. La variante que l'esprit de Mgr. Knox inventa pour servir d'ex-libris aux livres de votre bibliothèque, *Je suis Prêté,* pourrait s'employer aussi pour définir ce qu'il y avait de plus ravissant dans la nature de Maurice Baring. Il se prêtait à ses amis. Cet Anglais qui parlait toutes les langues (et leur préféra la française), avait le génie de tout comprendre. S'il a désiré au dernier jour de sa vie que ce livre, qui garde d'un bout à l'autre l'accent d'une confidence et le ton d'un journal intime, fût publié en France, c'était pour y être compris. Ambition qui l'honore. Un critique anglais a pu dire du style de Maurice Baring qu'il est si pur qu'un lecteur superficiel pourrait croire qu'il n'a pas de style du tout. Cela l'apparente aux auteurs français qu'il aima le plus, à Racine, à La Fontaine, à Stendhal.

Au collège d'Eton, sur ces pelouses dont l'Histoire nous dit que c'est le lieu où se forme, une génération après l'autre, cette espèce d'Anglais qui gagnent les guerres, Maurice Baring a gagné d'abord un prix de français. Ce premier succès scolaire a marqué toute sa vie d'écrivain. Il suffira de lire un livre de lui auquel vont bien des preférénces: *Have You Anything to Declare?* (N'avez vous rien à déclarer?) où l'auteur s'imagine être questionné en arrivant aux douanes du Ciel, sur ce qu'il apporte au monde de l'esprit, en venant de la terre. Il cite alors les paroles de tout ceux qu'il reconnaît pour les maîtres de sa pensée, qui l'ont aidé à bien vivre, et par conséquent à mourir. Avec les Grecs et les Latins, les Français tiennent la première place. Cette anthologie annotée, qui fait suite à tant d'ouvrages, est à la base même de toute son œuvre, la fondation sur laquelle s'élèvent ses ravissantes architectures. Maurice Baring s'est prêté à bien des expériences; il a interprêté un grand nombre de poètes et d'écrivains; sa parfaite connaissance du russe, de l'allemand, du danois, de l'espagnol et de l'italien lui a permis d'explorer librement le riche domaine littéraire des autres peuples. Converti à la foi catholique, il a fait le bilan de son expérience humaine: il a déclaré que de tous les actes de sa vie, c'était le seul qu'il n'ait jamais regretté. Quand au début de ce mal dont il souffrait pendant dix ans avant d'en mourir (paralysis agitans), j'allais le voir dans sa maison de Rottingdean, au bord de la mer, c'était pour le remercier d'un petit poème qu'il m'avait envoyé, écrit d'une main tremblante. En épigraphe je trouvai un vers de Racine: "Princesse en qui le ciel mit un esprit si doux." Je lui portais une lettre de celui qui fut le meilleur de ses amis français: l'abbé Mugnier.

Vous aviez dépêché Maurice Baring à notre rencontre, ma chère Laure, et vous l'aviez désigné pour nous servir de guide, en ce jour à jamais présent à ma mémoire, où sur votre invitation, ce prêtre qu'on nommait l'aumônier des Lettres françaises et moi avons franchi le seuil de votre maison. Notre amitié avait pris, depuis ce jour, ces nuances imperceptibles d'abord qui font sentir au voyageur nocturne que l'aube est au bout du paysage. Maurice Baring nous avait amenés chez vous, dans le lieu même qui allait devenir pour lui le pays de l'éternel matin.

Marthe Bibesco.